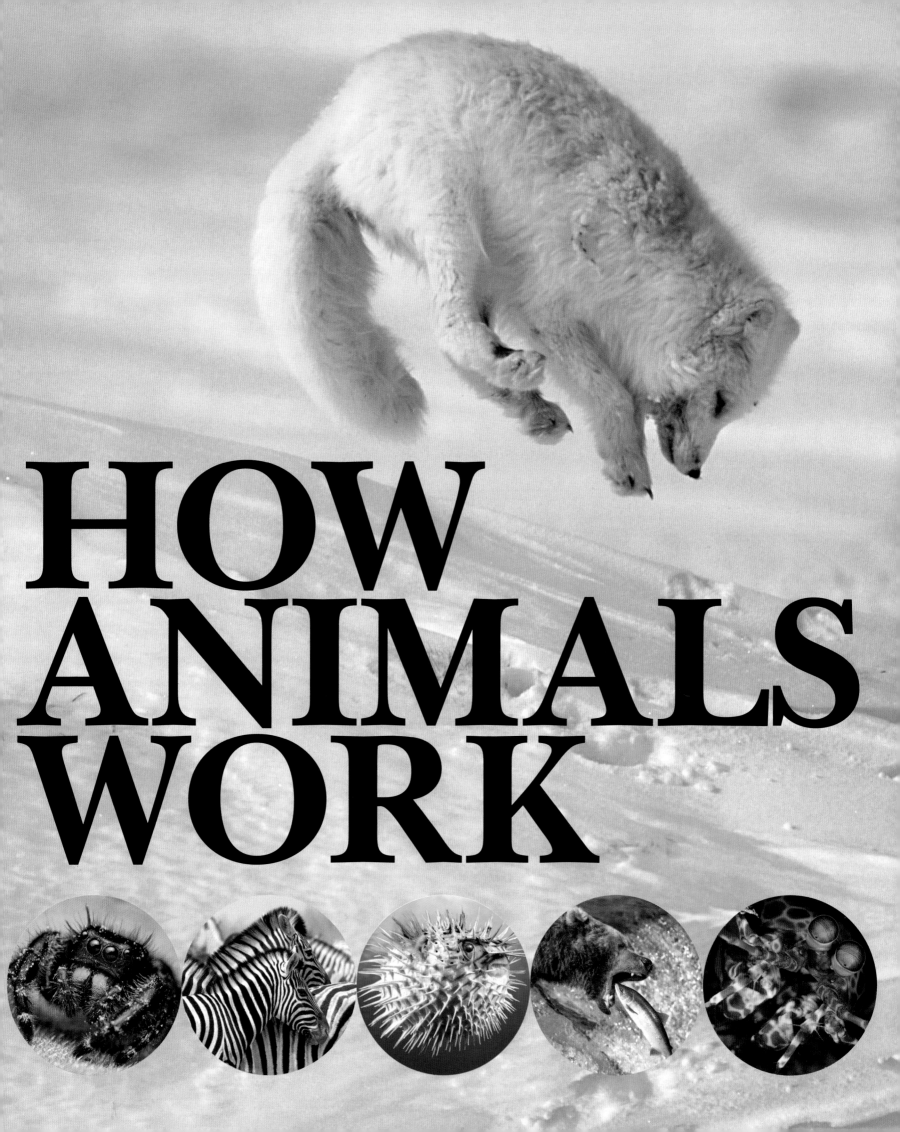

HOW
ANIMALS
WORK

**LONDON, NEW YORK,
MELBOURNE, MUNICH, and DELHI**

Consultant Dr. Kim Bryan

Senior editor Dr. Rob Houston
Project editor Jane Yorke
Editor Jessamy Wood
Designers Sarah Hilder, Mark Lloyd,
Joanne Mitchell, Liz Sephton, Smiljka Surla
US editor Margaret Parrish
Managing editor Julie Ferris
Managing art editor Owen Peyton Jones
Art director Martin Wilson
Publishing manager Andrew Macintyre
Category publisher Laura Buller
Picture researcher Laura Barwick
Illustrations KJA-artists.com
Production controller Charlotte Oliver
Production editor Sean Daly

First published in the United States in 2010
by DK Publishing
375 Hudson Street, New York, New York 10014

DK books are available at special discounts when purchased in bulk for
sales promotions, premiums, fundraising, or educational use. For details, contact:
DK Publishing Special Markets
375 Hudson Street
New York, New York 10014
SpecialSales@dk.com

A catalog record for this book
is available from the Library of Congress

ISBN: 978-0-7566-5897-7

Color reproduction by MDP, UK
Printed and bound by LEO Paper Products Ltd., China

**Discover more at
www.dk.com**

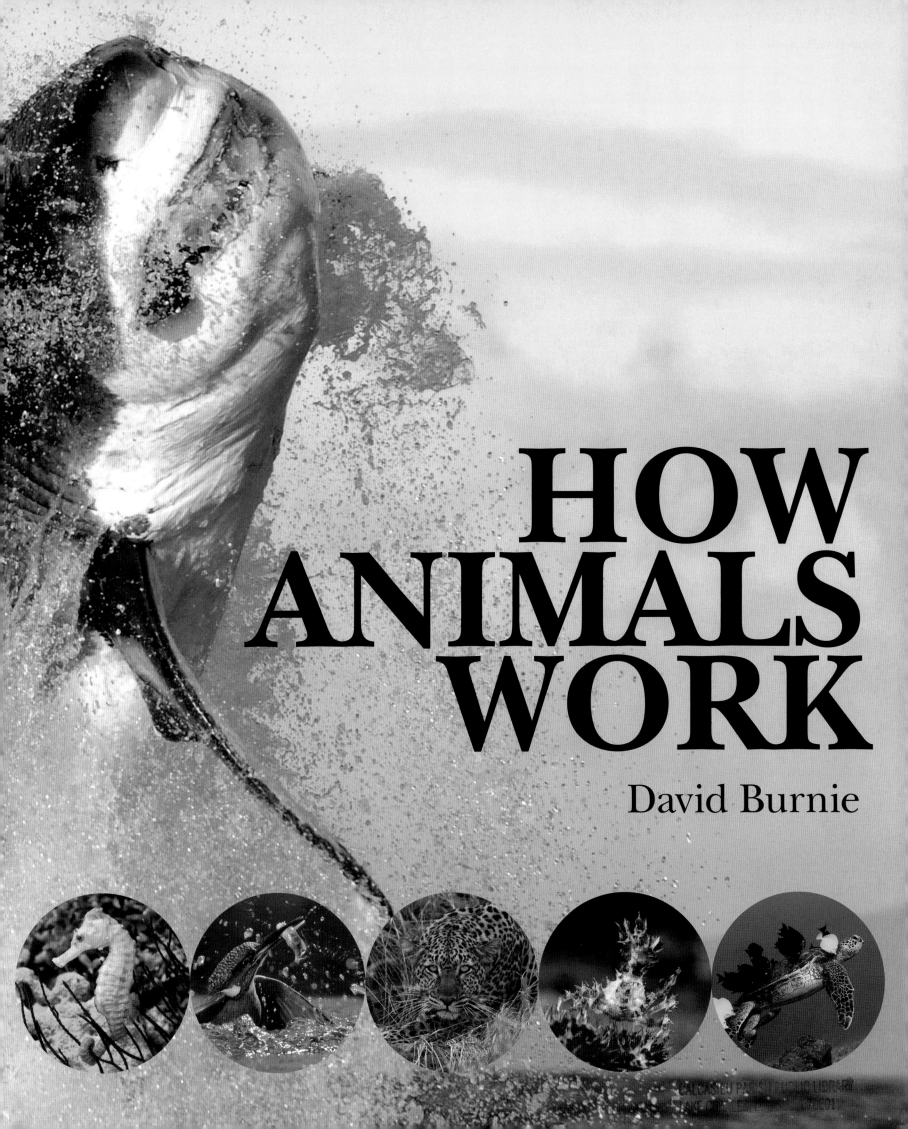

HOW ANIMALS WORK

David Burnie

Contents

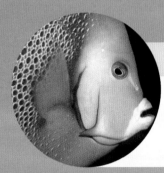

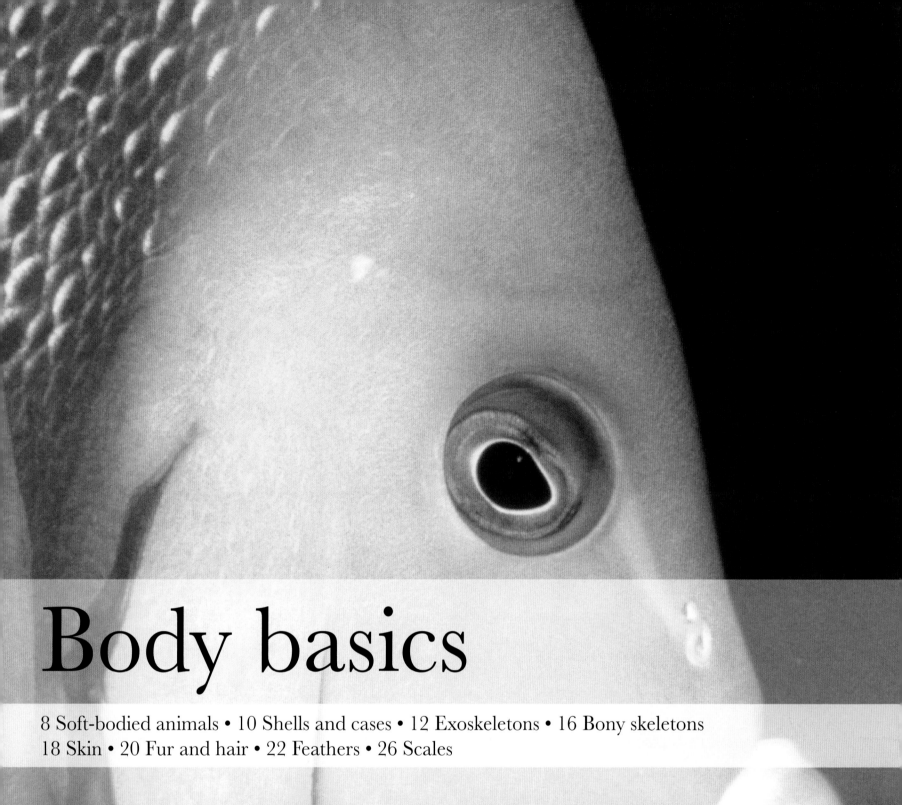

Body basics

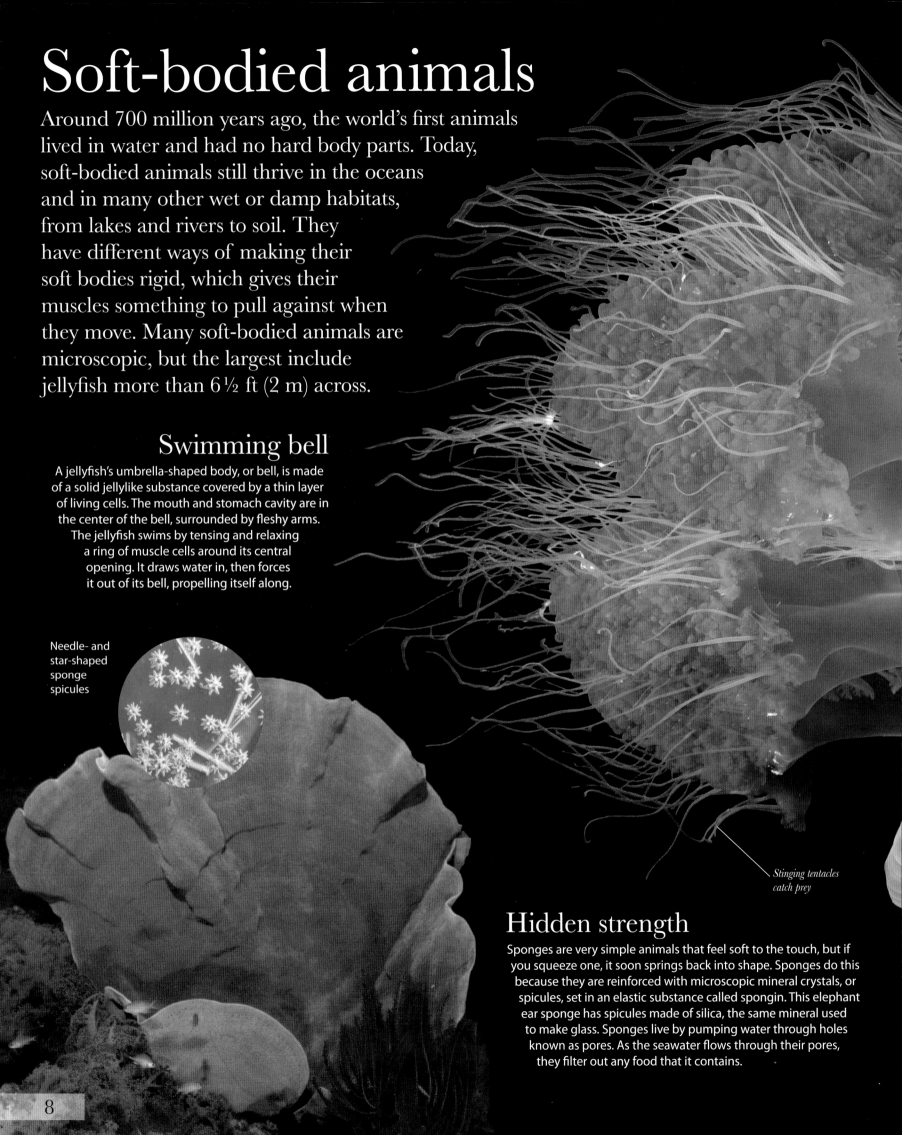

Soft-bodied animals

Around 700 million years ago, the world's first animals lived in water and had no hard body parts. Today, soft-bodied animals still thrive in the oceans and in many other wet or damp habitats, from lakes and rivers to soil. They have different ways of making their soft bodies rigid, which gives their muscles something to pull against when they move. Many soft-bodied animals are microscopic, but the largest include jellyfish more than 6 ½ ft (2 m) across.

Swimming bell

A jellyfish's umbrella-shaped body, or bell, is made of a solid jellylike substance covered by a thin layer of living cells. The mouth and stomach cavity are in the center of the bell, surrounded by fleshy arms. The jellyfish swims by tensing and relaxing a ring of muscle cells around its central opening. It draws water in, then forces it out of its bell, propelling itself along.

Needle- and star-shaped sponge spicules

Stinging tentacles catch prey

Hidden strength

Sponges are very simple animals that feel soft to the touch, but if you squeeze one, it soon springs back into shape. Sponges do this because they are reinforced with microscopic mineral crystals, or spicules, set in an elastic substance called spongin. This elephant ear sponge has spicules made of silica, the same mineral used to make glass. Sponges live by pumping water through holes known as pores. As the seawater flows through their pores, they filter out any food that it contains.

Jellyfish bell full of water

Living together

This sea fan is not just one animal, but a branching colony containing thousands of tiny coral animals called polyps. Each polyp has a soft body, which sits in a bright red case. The cases are cemented together, forming the branches of the fan. Sea fan polyps have flexible cases, but reef-building corals have much harder ones made from calcium carbonate—the same mineral found in chalk.

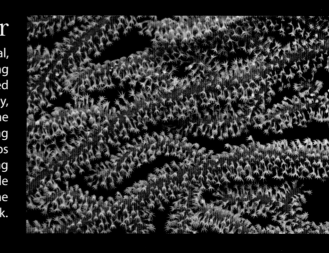

Pumped up

Earthworms have soft bodies that are divided into fluid-filled segments, and each one is kept under pressure, like a tire. This makes an earthworm's body firm enough to burrow through soil. The worms move by expanding and contracting their body segments in a series of muscular waves (see p. 46).

Inside a sea anemone

Sea anemones are related to jellyfish and corals, and their bodies share the same plan, with a ring of stinging tentacles surrounding a central mouth. The mouth opens into a hollow space where the anemone digests its food. A sucker usually fastens the anemone to rocks, although some anemones have a rounded base that anchors them in sand.

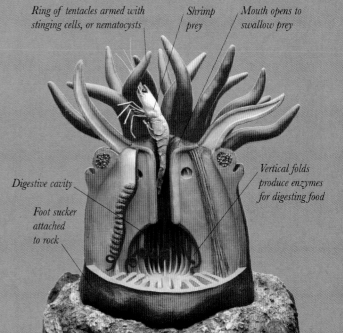

Ring of tentacles armed with stinging cells, or nematocysts

Shrimp prey

Mouth opens to swallow prey

Digestive cavity

Foot sucker attached to rock

Vertical folds produce enzymes for digesting food

A soft start

Many animals start life with soft bodies, which become tougher as they grow up. These young scorpions, riding on their mother's back, have a soft outer "skin" or body case. Each time they shed their skin, or molt, a thicker and harder skin develops in its place.

Shells and cases

A shell functions as both a skeleton and a mobile home. It keeps an animal in shape and helps protect the soft parts of its body. Shells also stop animals from drying out on land, including sea creatures that are exposed at low tide. The most common shelled animals are mollusks. They take chalky minerals out of the water around them, or from their food, then deposit them in layers, building up a thick, strong shell.

Twisted homes

Snails and their relatives usually have coiled shells with a clockwise twist. Extra turns are added to the shell as the snail grows, so that the animal always has enough space to pull its body safely inside.

Hinged shields

Scallops and other bivalves are mollusks with a two-part shell. These two parts, or valves, are held together by strong muscles and a flexible hinge. When bivalves feed, they open up their shells, but if danger threatens, most kinds close up tight. Scallops react differently. By clapping the two halves of their shells together and forcing out jets of water, they can swim to safety in rapid jerks.

Layer of tissue, or mantle, lining shell

Hidden chambers

A nautilus has a spiral-shaped shell, but with a different internal plan from a snail's. It is divided into separate compartments sealed by partition walls. The animal lives in the largest of these, which opens to the outside. The other shell compartments are filled with gas, and the nautilus uses them to adjust its depth in the water when swimming.

Chain mail

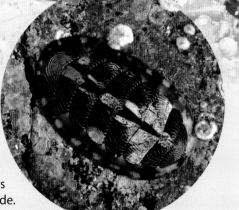

Chitons are unusual mollusks with flat shells made up of eight overlapping plates called valves. Surrounded by a rubbery "skirt," the valves are connected by hinges, which allow a chiton to bend as it slides over rocks. If a chiton is dislodged, it can curl up in its chain-mail shell to protect its soft underside.

Storm protection

Limpet shells are among the toughest in the animal world. Their conical shape withstands being battered by the waves and also fends off predatory birds. At low tide, these mollusks clamp their shells firmly to the hollows that they grind in rocks. When the tide is high, limpets creep over rocky shores feeding on algae, but they always return to the same spot before the water recedes.

Echinoderm cases

Echinoderms, such as sea urchins and starfish, have small chalky plates set in the outer layer of their skin. A starfish's plates are connected by muscles, which enable its five arms to flex and bend. A sea urchin's plates fit together to form a rigid case called a test, protected by a covering of sharp spines.

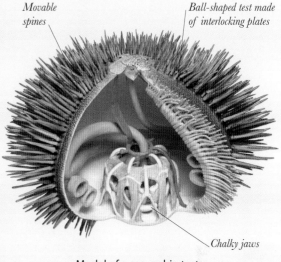

Movable spines

Ball-shaped test made of interlocking plates

Chalky jaws

Model of a sea urchin test

Upper valve with thick ridges for added strength

Row of simple eyes

Cuttlebone

Inner strength

Unlike the shells of other mollusks, a cuttlefish's shell is hidden inside its body. Known as a cuttlebone, this flat, chalky shell acts as a gas-filled float. A cuttlefish can change the amount of gas in the float, letting it rise through the water when swimming or sink to the seabed. Squid have similar internal shells, known as pens.

Exoskeletons

Arthropods, including insects, spiders, crustaceans, and centipedes, make up more than four-fifths of the world's animals. All of these creatures have an exoskeleton—an outer body case with flexible joints. Exoskeletons are built from chitin, a substance that resembles a natural plastic, together with minerals that provide extra strength. Exoskeletons are extremely good at withstanding wear and tear. Their main disadvantage is that they cannot enlarge once they have formed. To get around this problem, arthropods shed, or molt, the outer layer of their exoskeletons as they grow.

Tough plates fused together form boxlike head

Powerful mandibles used to fight rival males

Armored protection

Brandishing their huge, antlerlike jaws, or mandibles, two male stag beetles prepare to do battle. As with all insects, these rival beetles have an exoskeleton made of tough chitin plates with joints that allow their bodies to move. The hardened forewings, called elytra, cover and protect their transparent hind wings and their large mandibles are hollow, which saves on weight. In spite of all this body armor, stag beetles fly well, although not very fast.

Chest, or thorax, casing protects wing and leg muscles

Hardened forewings, or elytra, protect rear body, or abdomen

Body segments

An arthropod's body is divided into jointed segments. In centipedes, these segments are repeated along the length of the body. Each one is surrounded by hard body plates. These provide anchorage for the centipede's internal muscles, including those that reach into the legs.

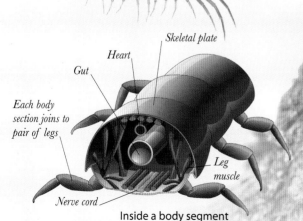

Each segment hinges with its neighbors, allowing body to bend

Skeletal plate

Heart

Gut

Each body section joins to pair of legs

Leg muscle

Nerve cord

Inside a body segment

Tubular leg with five joints

Exoskeleton outer layer, or cuticle, contains shiny, waterproofing wax

Discarded, hollow cuticle, complete with body hairs

New coat

Hanging upside down by a thread of silk, this golden orb-web spider has just shed, or molted, the outer "cuticle" layer of its exoskeleton. Molting is a complex operation, and it begins when a spider's old cuticle separates from the new one growing beneath. The old cuticle splits along the back, and the spider climbs out, extracting its legs like someone pulling their fingers from a glove. Some arthropods molt throughout their lives, but most insects stop molting once they have become adults with fully working wings.

Spider expands as new cuticle dries and hardens

Cover up

A grasshopper's exoskeleton covers every part of its body, including its antennae, its eyes, and even its breathing tubes, or tracheae. These tubes reach deep inside the grasshopper's body. Their linings are shed with the rest of the cuticle, each time the grasshopper molts.

Holes, or spiracles, leading into tracheae

Close-up of spiracles

Male's abdomen clasps female

Female's abdomen bends forward to make contact with male

Underwater giant

The Japanese spider crab is the world's largest arthropod, with a maximum leg span of nearly 13 ft (4 m). Like other crustaceans, it has a calcified exoskeleton—one that is reinforced with the mineral calcium carbonate. It has a shield, called a carapace, which protects its head, and powerful claws that can crack open shells. On land, without water to support its weight, the spider crab can barely move.

Elegant embrace

Locked together in a typical mating wheel position, these damselflies show how flexible exoskeletons can be. Their long abdomens are made up of many jointed sections that enable the male to arch its body and clasp the female behind the head during mating.

Holed up

Peering out of a hole in the reef, a coral hermit crab waves its feathery antennae to collect food. Unlike crabs that live in the open, this finger-sized crustacean has a long, soft abdomen. The hermit crab protects its body by living in an abandoned hole made by a tube worm in the coral. Every few months, the crab grows too big for its current home and has to search for new lodgings. This is a dangerous time, so the crab often explores at night, when there is less risk of being seen and attacked by predators.

Bony skeletons

The world's biggest animals—and most of the fastest—have internal skeletons made of bone. Bony skeletons are light and extremely strong. They form an inner framework for muscles to pull against, and they move at flexible joints. Bone is a living tissue, which means that this kind of skeleton can grow in step with the rest of an animal's body, and it can repair itself, although fractures take time to heal. Bony skeletons are found in all vertebrates, but in no other animals. Despite huge differences in size and shape, these skeletons share the same basic features—all have a backbone and most have four limbs.

Backbone of more than 40 individual bones, or vertebrae, separated by pads of cartilage

Harbor seal

Hip joint anchors rear legs to backbone

Thick, short thigh bone, or femur

Rib cage protects some of the soft internal body organs

Vertebrae and ribs fixed to upper part of shell

Stiff back

A tortoise has the same framework of bones as most other vertebrates, but the central part of its backbone is permanently joined to its shell. The armored shell is made up of bony scales called scutes, which are fused together and protect the tortoise from attack.

Curvy spine

All bony skeletons have a flexible backbone, or spine, which is made up of many separate bones called vertebrae. At the joints where vertebrae meet, the spine bends. Land mammals usually have fewer than 60 vertebrae, but snakes can have more than 400, letting them twist their bodies into coils and curves.

Rear flipper, made up of many small bones and joints, provides most of the power when swimming

Small movements between interlocking vertebrae form smooth curves in spine

16

Flexible framework

A harbor seal's skeleton has more than 200 different bones, which meet at junctions called joints. Some bones—particularly in the skull—are fused together, so that the joints are fixed and cannot move. Other bones are tipped with slippery cartilage where they join, which enables the bones to move smoothly against one another. Altogether, the skeleton makes up less than one-tenth of the seal's total weight.

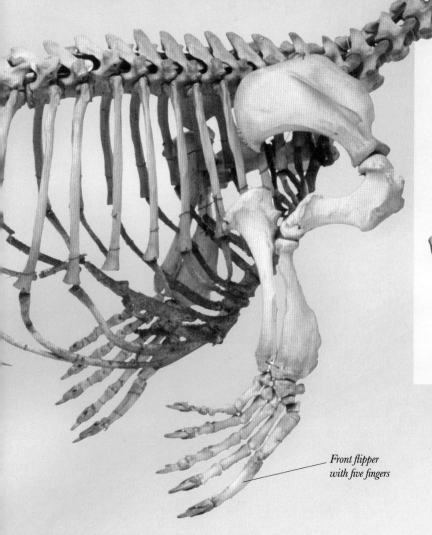

Front flipper with five fingers

Skulls

Big brain case
Compared to most other vertebrates, mammals have a large brain case, or cranium. Mammals are the only vertebrates that have differently shaped teeth, which they use for cutting, gripping, and grinding up food.

Cranium made up of several bones fused together

Hinged beak
Birds' beaks are made of bone covered by keratin—the same substance found in feathers and claws. In some birds, such as parrots, both halves of the beak hinge against the skull, allowing the birds to open their mouths wide when feeding.

Parrot's double-hinged beak opens wide for feeding

Large jaws
A crocodile's jaw is made of several bones fused together. Unlike mammals, this reptile has conical teeth that it continually sheds and replaces during its lifetime.

Anchorage for jaw muscles

Crocodile's conical teeth tear up meat

Lightweight skeleton

Animals with bony skeletons all have gristle, or cartilage, in their joints. Sharks, skates, and rays, however, are different. Although they are vertebrates, their entire skeletons are made of cartilage, instead of bone. This kind of cartilaginous skeleton is not as strong as a bony one, but it is much lighter. Even so, open-water sharks often swim continuously, partly to keep themselves afloat.

Long-legged runner

This wolf skeleton has the same limb bones as those of a harbor seal, but their proportions are very different. The wolf's main leg bones are much longer than the seal's, while its toes are shorter—two adaptations that make the wolf a fast and tireless runner.

Ankle held off ground

Only toes touch ground when running

Flick of the fingers

A bat's wings are made of skin, stretched out by extremely long and slender finger bones. During flight, a bat can quickly change direction by flexing its eight fingers and giving the wing tips an extra flick as they beat up and down.

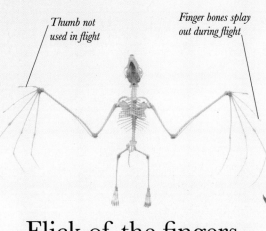

Thumb not used in flight

Finger bones splay out during flight

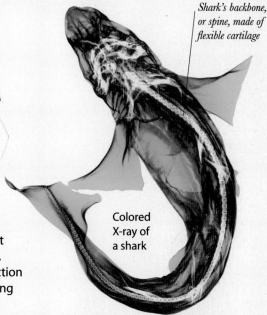

Shark's backbone, or spine, made of flexible cartilage

Colored X-ray of a shark

Skin

All vertebrates have skin, although it is often hidden from view by a layer of fur, feathers, or scales. However, in some animals, skin is the main protective barrier between the body and the outside world. This flexible body covering carries out many different tasks, such as keeping water in and germs out and helping animals to communicate or to hide. Skin is one of the fastest-growing parts of the body. It needs to be, because few other organs get so much wear and tear.

Common dolphin

Glands keep skin moist and exude poison onto its surface

Amphibian skin

Unlike human skin, amphibian skin has glands that ooze slippery mucus onto its surface. Many amphibians also have poison glands. These can be scattered across their bodies or concentrated in places where predators are most likely to bite. Oxygen is absorbed through the skin into the surface blood vessels, while carbon dioxide travels in the opposite direction.

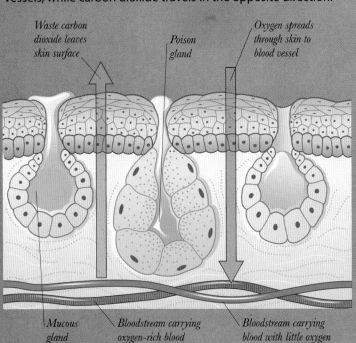

Waste carbon dioxide leaves skin surface

Poison gland

Oxygen spreads through skin to blood vessel

Mucous gland

Bloodstream carrying oxygen-rich blood

Bloodstream carrying blood with little oxygen

Skin on show

Clinging to a plant stem, an Ivory Coast running frog shows off its extraordinarily vivid skin. These brilliant colors are a warning to predators, showing that its skin is smeared with poisons produced by special glands. This amphibian's skin is moist and paper-thin, and it can absorb oxygen, helping the frog to breathe both on land and when under water. The frog also has an area of absorbent skin on its underside called a seat patch, through which it can drink when sitting in a puddle. To keep its skin in good condition, the frog sheds the outer layer every few days and swallows the dead skin cells.

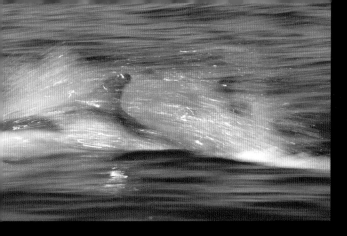

Slippery skin

Fish make their bodies slimy with mucus, but dolphins reduce drag by scattering skin cells as they speed through the sea. Dolphin skin also ripples with the water, making dolphins a hundred times more slippery than a human swimmer.

Chemical factory

Many animals produce different chemical substances in their skin. Some of the chemicals help to defend animals against predators. Other secretions help to protect an animal's body against the effects of their environment.

Wartlike bumps called parotoid glands ooze poisonous chemicals

Poisonous surface

The fire salamander secretes poison onto its skin to deter predators. The poisons are made in the parotoid glands, which are the two rows of bumps along the salamander's back and the pair of bumps behind its eyes.

Self-repair

This lion's face was cut during a fight. Skin often gets damaged—either during skirmishes or by accident. Once this happens, the injury soon begins to heal. A blood clot forms over the damaged area, and skin cells start to multiply, forming a scar. Unlike normal skin, scar tissue is harder and less flexible, with fewer blood vessels and nerves.

Scar tissue lacks fur

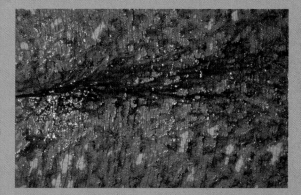

Natural sunscreen

Hippopotamus skin produces droplets of oil that screen the ultraviolet rays in sunshine. This oil also helps to fight waterborne bacteria that can infect a hippopotamus's wounds when wallowing in water.

Practical protection

Vultures may not look beautiful, but having bare skin on their heads and necks is ideal for their scavenging way of life. It allows the birds to put their heads inside a carcass without getting their feathers covered in blood. Like all vertebrates, a vulture's skin has two main layers. The deepest one, called the dermis, contains blood vessels and nerves. The layer above it, called the epidermis, produces a constant supply of dead cells containing a protein called keratin. These dead cells form a waterproof barrier on the skin's surface.

Sleeping bag

At sunset, some parrotfish hide away in rock crevices and secrete a mucus cocoon from their skin. This jellylike blanket probably masks their scent, making it harder for predators and parasites to find the fish as they sleep.

Fur and hair

Invertebrates sometimes look furry, but only mammals have real fur and hair. A fur coat protects against the heat and the cold, and it often works as camouflage. On some mammals, fur can be amazingly dense—sea otters have about 1 million hairs on every square inch (150,000 hairs per sq cm) of their bodies, which is as many as most people have on their entire heads. Hairs grow in small pits, or follicles, in the skin. Each follicle contains a tiny muscle and when this contracts, an animal's fur stands up on end.

Changing coats

Many woodland mammals change the color of their coats as they grow up. Wild boar piglets are born with brown-and-yellow-striped coats, which fade to a darker brown by the time they are five months old. Young deer, or fawns, have spotted coats at birth. In many species, these disappear by the time a fawn is one year old. The stripes and spots act as camouflage, helping to conceal the young in the sun-dappled shade under the trees.

Long guard hairs form coat surface

Close-up of fur layers

Underfur traps air, conserving warmth

Piglet's coloring contrasts with mother's dark, bristly coat

Winter layers

Huddling together on the Alaskan tundra, these hardy musk oxen are wearing their warm winter coats. The dark-brown, outer fur layer is made up of extra-long guard hairs (see p. 122), which protect the oxen from the snow and gale-force winter winds. Beneath this coarse, shaggy layer grows a shorter, woolly undercoat called underfur—one of the lightest and warmest in the animal world. Like many hoofed mammals, musk oxen molt their coats twice a year and grow a shorter, cooler coat for the summer months.

Long bristles deter insect-eating birds and parasitic wasps

Tiger moth caterpillar

Fake fur

Insects and spiders often have furlike bristles on parts of their bodies. Instead of being made of keratin, these hairs are made of chitin—the substance that forms insect exoskeletons. Large moths and bumblebees have coats of bristles that keep their flight muscles warm, but caterpillars use theirs mainly for self-defense. Caterpillar bristles may look harmless, but when touched, they break easily and release poisonous chemicals that help to ward off predators.

Furry wet suit

When an otter dives, its outer fur gets wet, but its skin stays completely dry. This happens because, like many land mammals, the otter has a double coat. This Asian small-clawed otter's long guard hairs form the coat's surface. They point from the head toward the tail, creating a streamlined shape for swimming. The otter's underfur hairs are finer and much more densely packed. They are also kinked, which helps to trap a layer of air. This air keeps water out and ensures that the otter's body stays warm and dry.

Arctic protection

Polar bears can survive the bitter cold on the Arctic's drifting ice and in the sea. They have a thick fur coat and an insulating layer of fat, called blubber, which protects against the freezing temperatures.

Hair's hollow center traps air

Hollow hairs
This microscopic view of polar bear fur shows that its guard hairs are hollow and filled with air. These hairs work like an insulating jacket and greatly reduce heat loss, helping to keep the bear's internal body temperature at 98.6°F (37°C).

Camouflage colors

Crouching in dry grass, a female leopard is camouflaged from prey by its beautifully patterned coat. Spotted markings like these are created mainly by melanin—a chemical pigment stored in individual hairs. Melanin can produce a wide range of hues, from pale yellow to brown and black. This pigment also occurs in animal skin and in many other body coverings, such as feathers and scales.

Stripes of dark and light colors blend in with woodland surroundings

Heat portrait
This infrared photograph reveals the surface temperature of a polar bear's body. The white and yellow areas are coldest, proving that the bear has good body insulation. Exposed body parts, such as the nose, look red and show where the bear is losing the most heat.

Feathers

Birds are the only animals that have feathers and without them, they would be unable to fly. However, feathers have many other important uses. They help keep birds warm and dry, and they can also play a vital part in courtship displays and in camouflage. Feathers are made of keratin—the same substance that forms hair—and they grow from a bird's skin. Birds can have more than 25,000 feathers, from the soft down feathers covering their bodies, to the long flight feathers in their wings and tails.

Blade, or vane, of flight feather pushes against air when wing beats down

Contour feathers streamline bird's body shape

Covert feathers smooth airflow over wing

Primary flight feathers help bird steer

Graylag goose

Flight formation

Speeding over the Amazon Rain forest, two red-and-green macaws show off their dazzling plumage. Like all flying birds, they get their smooth body outline from contour feathers, which overlap to create a streamlined shape. The bird's flight feathers are arranged in precise rows on the wings. The longest feathers, known as primaries, lie at the outer edge of each wing. Smaller feathers, called coverts, are arranged over the base of the flight feathers, helping to create lift as the wings move through the air.

Bath time

Water literally rolls off a duck's back—and off this goose's, too. This happens because contour feathers have microscopic scales that form a water-repellent surface, just like some artificial fabrics. Birds also use their beaks to waterproof their feathers by covering them with oils from their preen gland. Cormorants are the only birds that soak up water when they dive to catch fish. Once back on land, they open up their wings to dry the feathers.

Feather types

Flat vane

Soft filaments

Stiff quill

Down feather
With their fluffy filaments, down feathers trap a layer of warm air next to a bird's skin and help to cushion and protect its body.

Contour feather
These feathers have soft filaments at their base and flat tips that overlap to give the bird's body a streamlined surface.

Flight feather
The smooth vane of a flight feather is very light with a central, rigid spine, or quill, bearing hundreds of tiny strands, called barbs.

Missing flight feathers

Running repairs

A bird's delicate plumage becomes tattered with use—the wing feathers, in particular, get a tremendous amount of wear and tear. To stay in top condition, birds shed, or molt, their feathers regularly and grow new ones in their place. Like most birds, this wedge-tailed eagle molts its flight feathers in a set pattern, a few at a time. Water birds, however, often lose their flight feathers all at once. They cannot fly until their new feathers have grown back, so the birds molt in remote places, staying a safe distance from predators on the shore.

All zipped up

Viewed up close, this Eurasian jay's flight feather looks like a comb with tiny teeth, or barbs, set in neat rows that almost touch. The barbs are armed with smaller branches, called barbules, which lock together with flexible hooks. The barbs and interlocking barbules make up the feather's flat surface, known as the vane, and enable the feather to bend and stretch as the wing beats up and down in flight.

Microscopic view of interlocking barbules

Colorful display

Birds include some of the most brilliantly colored animals in the natural world. In many species, such as these birds of paradise, the males use their striking plumage as a signal to attract a mate. Most feather colors are produced by chemical pigments, which are stored inside a bird's feathers as they grow. Shiny, or iridescent, colors—like those of the hummingbird (see p. 40)—are created in a different way, when light reflects off the microscopic structures on the surface of feathers.

Flushed with color

With its beak tucked under its bright pink wing, a flamingo takes time off from feeding. This wading bird gets its colorful plumage from the food it eats. There are chemical pigments called carotenoids in the microorganisms and shrimp that the flamingo filters from salty lakes. These pigments circulate in the bird's blood until they reach the feather-forming cells in its skin. Here, the pink color is built into new feathers, which grow to replace those that are shed when the flamingo molts.

Scales

Many different animals have a flexible body covering of scaly skin. Scales are small, tough plates that grow from the skin in neat patterns. They give body protection and also help some animals to move. Insect scales are made of chitin, like the rest of their exoskeletons. The scales of vertebrates are made of hard substances such as dentine, which is also found in teeth, and the protein keratin, which also makes up claws and fingernails. Animals with the strongest scales include crocodiles, whose scales are reinforced with bone.

Cutting edge

It may look like a walking pine cone, but this scaly animal is actually a tropical mammal called a pangolin. Its scales are thin but hard-edged, and the pangolin curls up and raises them if it is attacked. Newborn pangolins have soft scales, but these start to harden after a few days. Once a pangolin is fully grown, its scales are kept sharp by wear and tear as it moves around in the forest trees.

Newly revealed cuticle with a glossy sheen

Old skin peels away from head backward

Scaly jacket

Scales surround a fish's body like a tight-fitting jacket, helping it to slip easily through the ocean. Fish living in the open sea often have scaly skin with a silvery sheen, whereas species from coastal waters and coral reefs are usually brilliantly colored. Growth rings on the scales of bony fish can be used to estimate a fish's age.

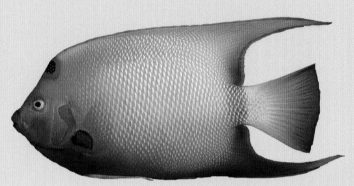

Angelfish

Shedding skin

Snake skin has a thin outer layer, or cuticle, which is very smooth to the touch. The cuticle does not stretch and must be cast off so that the animal can grow. Snakes shed their whole cuticle in one piece, pulling it inside out by rubbing their bodies against rough objects.

Sandpaper skin

If a shark's skin is rubbed the wrong way, it feels as rough as sandpaper—at one time, people used it for exactly this purpose. Unlike other fish, a shark's body is covered in tiny toothlike scales. Known as denticles, they reduce turbulence in the water, letting sharks close in silently on their prey.

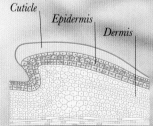

Microscopic view of shark's denticles

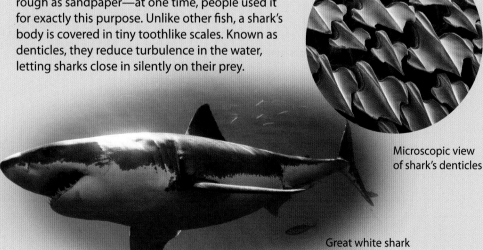

Great white shark

Scale structure

All scales are fixed in skin, but they are made of different materials and grow in different ways.

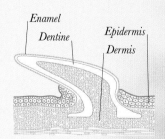

Enamel
Dentine
Epidermis
Dermis

Cuticle
Epidermis
Dermis

Shark scale

A shark's scales are made of dentine and enamel—hard tissues found in teeth—and are anchored in the deepest layer of the skin, or dermis. Each scale has a working life of a few weeks. After this, it is replaced.

Snake scale

The scales of snakes and lizards grow on the epidermis—the outer layer of the skin. They can lie flat or overlap in rows. These scales last for life, although their outer cuticle is shed several times a year.

Overlapping tiles

To the naked eye, the wings of this peacock butterfly look smooth and velvety. However, closer examination under a microscope reveals a covering of tiny scales, which are arranged in overlapping rows, like tiles on a roof. A butterfly's scales are flat and hollow, and they give the wings their magnificent color.

Head scales caked with salt sprayed from glands near eyes

Background wing color produced by pigments in scales

Iridescent eye spots created by reflective scales

Tiny ridges on surface of scales reflect light, producing different colors

Microscopic view of butterfly scales

Scary scales

The marine iguana has large scales on its head that form different shapes, such as knobs and cones, and a crest of spike-shaped scales running down its back. Despite its fearsome appearance, it is a harmless vegetarian, feeding entirely on seaweed.

Snake's eye protected by a single, clear scale, or spectacle

Slippery scales

Snakes have smooth scales, arranged in diagonal rows. Their belly scales are larger and set in horizontal rows to help them slide across the ground. Other reptiles, including crocodiles, tortoises, and some lizards, have armored, bony scales called scutes. In giant tortoises, shell scutes can be nearly 10 in (25 cm) across.

Animals on the move

Creeping and sliding

Everything moves in the living world, including plants that turn to follow the sun, and aquatic bacteria that maneuver through the seas. However, animals not only move faster than other life forms, but they also do it in the most amazing variety of ways. They creep, run, swim, and fly, using a huge range of body parts, from muscular suckers to feather-covered wings. Animals that creep and slide often score low marks for speed, but some snakes reach 13 mph (20 kph) over short distances, an impressive achievement for animals without legs.

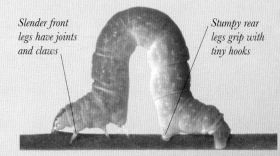

Slender front legs have joints and claws

Stumpy rear legs grip with tiny hooks

In the loop

Looper caterpillars get their name from their unusual way of moving. This one has formed a loop and is about to stretch forward by releasing its front legs. Once it has straightened out, it grips with its front legs and releases its back ones, so the loop can re-form. By doing this repeatedly, it moves forward along the twig.

Arms and feet

Starfish and their relatives have hundreds of tube feet arranged in rows on the undersides of their arms. Each one is thinner than a matchstick and is tipped with a sticky sucker. On their own, these suckers are weak, but because the starfish has so many of them, they give it tremendous pulling power. Starfish use their tube feet to creep over rocks and to turn the right way up if they get dislodged by the waves. They also use them to pull open the shells of mussels and other bivalves, so that they can feed on the animals inside.

Magnified view of tube feet

Suckers and slime

Creeping across a pane of glass, this garden snail shows off its suckerlike foot. Many animals have suckers, but most use them just for holding on. A snail's foot not only sucks it to surfaces, but it also powers its motion. The movement is produced by the muscle fibers in the foot stretching and contracting in waves. Each wave starts at the tail end of the foot and moves forward to the head, pushing the snail along. To smooth its path, the snail produces lots of sticky mucus, which leaves a glistening trail. At top speed, a garden snail can move at 26 ft (8 m) per hour.

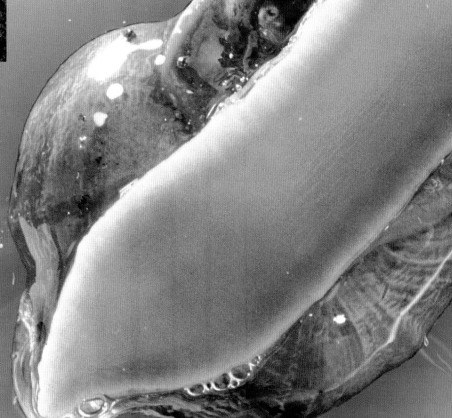

Slime reduces friction between foot and glass

*Eye on long tentacle
helps snail find its way*

*Wave of muscle
contraction moves
snail forward*

*Smell receptor used
for sensing food and
surroundings*

Multipurpose spines

This club urchin, which lives in the seas of New Zealand, "walks" over rocky seabeds by moving its colorful spines. The spines are stiff, but can swivel in any direction, since they are mounted on flexible joints. Sea urchins can also use their spines to grind burrows in rock or to jam themselves in crevices.

Staying put

These goose barnacles start their lives as tiny larvae, which use their feathery legs to swim near the surface of the sea. After months adrift, they change shape and fasten themselves to rocks. From that moment onward, they never move again. Instead of swimming to find food, they collect it as it drifts past. This way of life is shared by many invertebrates, from corals to giant clams.

How snakes slither

Snakes have four different ways of moving. Many use two or three methods, switching them to suit the ground they are traveling over and to match the speed they need. Sidewinding is a special kind of movement used by snakes that live in deserts and other habitats with loose ground.

Straight-line movement
When snakes creep in straight lines, they raise the scales on their undersides, moving them forward in waves. The scales push the snake forward when they touch the ground. This kind of movement is used by heavy snakes that have wide belly scales.

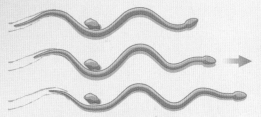

Serpentine movement
When a snake presses against an object with its side, it produces a backward thrust, which makes the snake slide forward. Most snakes use this kind of movement on land. Speeded up, they also use it when they swim, by pushing against the water.

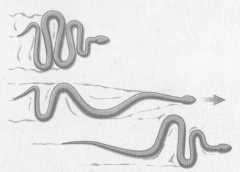

Accordion movement
On smooth ground, snakes often fold into curves. Using their tails as anchors, they reach forward with their heads and necks. The neck curves up, turning into the anchor, and the tail catches up. Snakes also use their coils as an anchor when they climb in trees.

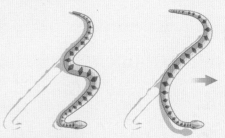

Sidewinding
Instead of crawling, a sidewinding snake lifts its head and neck and throws them sideways through the air. The rest of its body follows, while its head moves on again. Used by rattlesnakes and vipers, sidewinding leaves a series of J-shaped tracks in the sand.

Moving on legs

Legs work like levers, thrusting an animal forward and keeping its body off the ground. The earliest known land animals with legs were millipedes, which have been on earth for over 400 million years. These pioneers were joined by six-legged insects, and then by four-legged vertebrates, which left water for a life on land. At first, they were slow-moving animals, but evolution produced longer, stronger legs, making predators better at chasing their food and helping prey to escape. Today, many hoofed mammals can run at more than 30 mph (50 kph), although that is sluggish compared to a sprinting cheetah.

Killer sprint

The cheetah has a top speed of more than 68 mph (110 kph), thanks to its highly flexible spine, which arches up and down, extending its enormous stride. The cheetah hunts out in the open, accelerating from a standing start even faster than a car. However, a cheetah does not have great staying power. If the chase lasts more than a minute, it risks overheating, and its prey is usually able to escape.

Low slung

This spectacled salamander walks with its legs splayed out to the sides and its body slung close to the ground. Its body curls from side to side when it walks—a feature of movement that four-legged animals inherited from their fishy ancestors. Lizards also move in this sprawling way, but mammals have their legs under their bodies, which makes them the more efficient movers.

Splayed-out foot increases grip when walking up steep surfaces

Marathon mammals

Pronghorns are the fastest long-distance runners in the animal world. Their maximum speed is more than 53 mph (85 kph), but they can cruise across North America's open plains at 34 mph (55 kph) for more than 10 minutes without tiring. Pronghorns are able to do this because they have an unusually large heart and lungs and small hooves, which minimize contact with the ground. Although they look more like antelopes, their closest living relatives are actually giraffes.

Maximum legs

Millipedes have more legs than any other animal—up to an incredible 750. Their legs are tiny, and they have four on each body segment, unlike centipedes, which have two. When millipedes move, they push backward about 12 legs at a time in coordinated waves, which stops the legs from getting in each others' way.

Armored exoskeleton shields legs when millipede coils up

Legs move in waves that start at the head

Walking on water

With its legs spread wide, the raft spider runs across the surface of ponds, homing in on flying insects that have crash-landed in the water. It has water-repellent hairs on the surface of its feet, which stop it from sinking through the water's surface. It is not the only animal that moves in this way—water striders also use the water's surface as a hunting ground. Most of these little insects live on ponds and lakes, but in warm parts of the world, some even skate over the waves far out at sea.

Changing gaits

Hoofed mammals often use several different ways of moving, or gaits, which work like different gears. Zebras and their relatives have four natural gaits. Walking, the slowest, has a four-beat rhythm made by each leg landing one at a time. Trotting has two beats, with the legs moving in diagonal pairs. This is used to cover long distances efficiently. Cantering is quicker, with three beats, while galloping, with four, is the fastest and is used to evade predators. Trot, canter, and gallop have periods of "suspension," when all four feet are in the air.

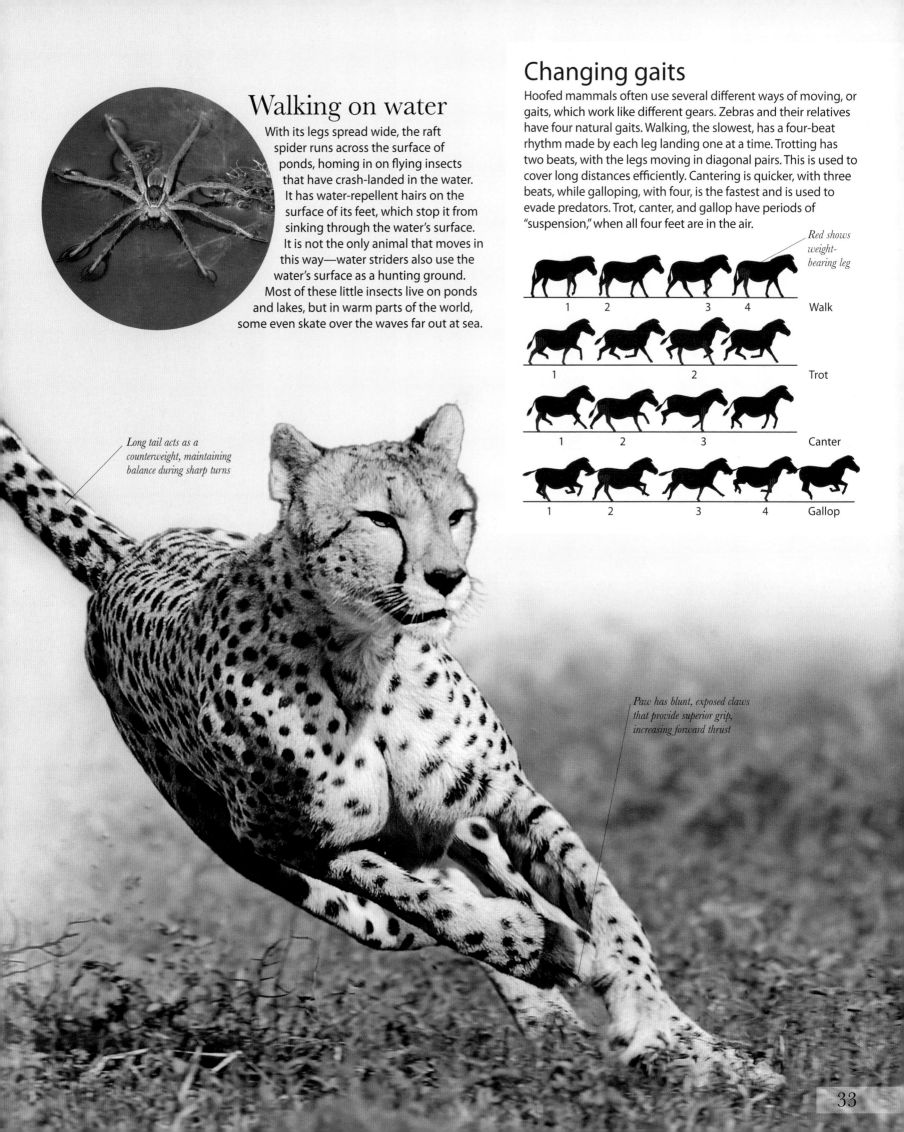

Red shows weight-bearing leg

1   2   3   4   Walk

1   2   Trot

1   2   3   Canter

1   2   3   4   Gallop

Long tail acts as a counterweight, maintaining balance during sharp turns

Paw has blunt, exposed claws that provide superior grip, increasing forward thrust

Jumping and climbing

The animal world contains some big kickers, as well as expert climbers. Many small animals jump to make a fast escape, but kangaroos can keep hopping for nearly a mile before they start to tire. Although climbing is a slower way of moving, it lets animals get food that is hard to reach. Some climbers come down to breed, but many spend their whole lives high above the ground.

Knee joint is straight at end of kick

Suckerlike toe pads grip leaf's surface

Tail is strong enough to support monkey's body

Fifth leg

A spider monkey's long tail works like an extra leg. Its tip is prehensile, meaning that it can curl around branches, and the inside has bare skin, giving it a nonslip grip. Spider monkeys live high up in the rain forest canopy. They can hang by just their tails when they feed.

Opposing toes close around branch

Liftoff!

With a powerful kick from its back legs, a red-eyed tree frog launches itself into the air. After liftoff, it spreads out its legs and toes, turning its body into a parachute as it sails through the air. Tree frogs have sticky toe-pads for getting a grip on leaves, and their forward-pointing eyes help them to judge distances before making a jump.

Holding tight

Climbing animals have many different ways of moving around without losing their grip.

Hooks

Lice are small insects that spend their lives aboard mammals and birds. Their legs end in sharp hooks that close around fur or feathers. To move, a louse releases its hooks in a set sequence, so that while some are moving, the rest are still holding tight.

Claws

Woodpeckers specialize in climbing tree trunks. Their claws dig in when they land on a tree, and their tails help to brace them when they feed. Woodpeckers can only climb upward, but nuthatches can climb both up and down without losing their grip.

Sticky toes

Geckos can climb almost any surface, including polished glass. They do this by using billions of microscopic bristles on the undersides of their toes. These stick to anything they touch. To move, a gecko carefully unpeels its toes, so that its bristles lose their grip.

Flexible fins

The mudskipper is an unusual fish that lives in mangrove swamps. It can breathe in air, and it can also "skip" and climb to catch its food. Mudskippers skip by flicking their tails. They climb by using fins that work like suckers and others that are like stubby legs.

Bright stripes revealed during mid-jump

Toes spread out to increase surface area

Front feet angle to touch down before back ones when frog lands

Flash of color when frog jumps startles predators, giving frog time to escape

Tree-climbing crab

The coconut crab is a climber with a leg span of around 3 ft (1 m). It hauls its massive body up coconut trees to reach nuts that are still soft and unripe. It uses its legs to grip the tree trunk while its claws cut into the fruit.

Leaps and bounds

For their size, the world's best jumpers are fleas. They can leap more than 12 in (30 cm), which is about 200 times their body length. Human athletes can manage around 29 ft (9 m), but the record jumpers are large kangaroos and snow leopards. They can leap more than 42 ft (13 m) on level ground.

Bushbaby

Human—world-record distance of 29 ft 4½ in (8.95 m) jumped by US athlete Mike Powell in 1991

Red kangaroo

Snow leopard

Southern cricket frog

Length (feet)

0   5   10   15   20   25   30   35   40   45

Leaping lemur

Kicking with its hind legs, a Verreaux's sifaka leaps
through the dry forest of southern Madagascar. This
agile lemur spends most of its life in trees, keeping its
body upright by clinging to the trunks. It stays upright
even when it jumps. Adults are powerful jumpers and
can clear up to 33 ft (10 m) in a single bound from one
tree to the next. On the ground, sifakas move like
someone jumping along a tightrope, with their bodies
standing straight and their arms held out for balance,
while they hop along sideways.

Gliding

Gliding animals are experts at taking off, but do not use muscle power to stay in the air, as flying animals do when they beat their wings. Gliders move through the air on outstretched wings, fins, limbs, or even flaps of skin. Some flying animals also glide—gliding birds can travel immense distances by riding on columns of rising air. Forest animals make shorter glides by jumping off from trees. In the air, they open skin flaps that act as parachutes, speeding them forward as they fall. At sea, flying fish can escape predators by gliding more than 1,000 ft (300 m) on their fins.

Skin flaps create a concave shape that creates lift like a wing

Leap in the dark

Spreading its legs wide, a southern flying squirrel glides between trees on flaps of elastic skin. The folds run from its wrists to its ankles, creating a surface that acts like a wing as it glides through the air. Once it has landed, the flaps tighten up along its sides, so that they do not get in the way as it climbs. Flying squirrels can glide up to 160 ft (50 m) at a time. They live in the forests of North America and, unlike typical squirrels, they feed at night.

Hind legs swing forward, bringing body into vertical position in preparation to land

Giant outstretched foot creates drag, slowing frog's fall

Fish out of water

After bursting out of the ocean, a flying fish speeds above the surface, gliding on its wing-shaped pectoral fins. Farther down its body, this fish also has a smaller pair of fins that help to keep it in the air. Flying fish have a rapid top speed of about 18 mph (30 kph) and they can glide several yards above the sea. A flying fish's tail works like an outboard motor. If the fish is being chased, it dips its tail into the water and flicks it quickly, accelerating the fish up into another glide.

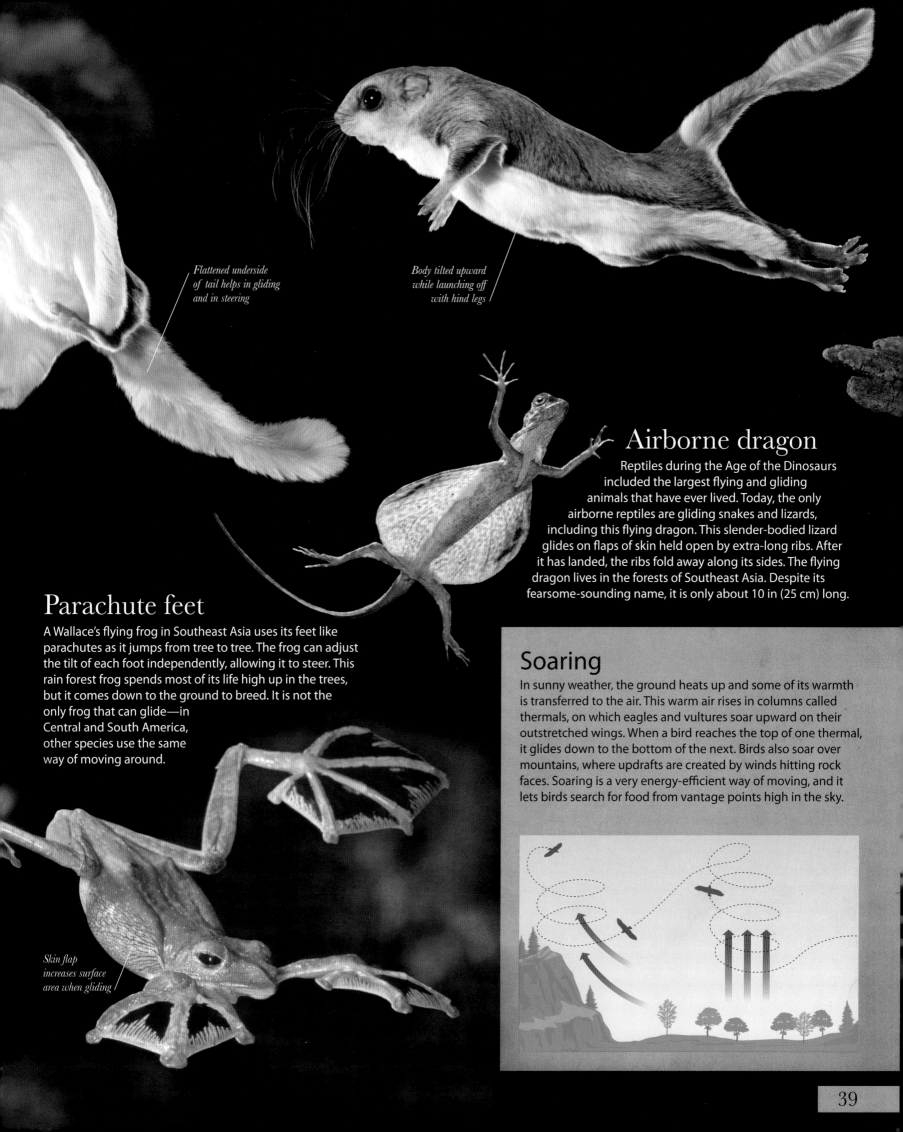

*Flattened underside
of tail helps in gliding
and in steering*

*Body tilted upward
while launching off
with hind legs*

Airborne dragon

Reptiles during the Age of the Dinosaurs included the largest flying and gliding animals that have ever lived. Today, the only airborne reptiles are gliding snakes and lizards, including this flying dragon. This slender-bodied lizard glides on flaps of skin held open by extra-long ribs. After it has landed, the ribs fold away along its sides. The flying dragon lives in the forests of Southeast Asia. Despite its fearsome-sounding name, it is only about 10 in (25 cm) long.

Parachute feet

A Wallace's flying frog in Southeast Asia uses its feet like parachutes as it jumps from tree to tree. The frog can adjust the tilt of each foot independently, allowing it to steer. This rain forest frog spends most of its life high up in the trees, but it comes down to the ground to breed. It is not the only frog that can glide—in Central and South America, other species use the same way of moving around.

*Skin flap
increases surface
area when gliding*

Soaring

In sunny weather, the ground heats up and some of its warmth is transferred to the air. This warm air rises in columns called thermals, on which eagles and vultures soar upward on their outstretched wings. When a bird reaches the top of one thermal, it glides down to the bottom of the next. Birds also soar over mountains, where updrafts are created by winds hitting rock faces. Soaring is a very energy-efficient way of moving, and it lets birds search for food from vantage points high in the sky.

Flying

Many animals can glide, but only birds, bats, and insects can flap their wings to stay in the air. Birds fly farthest and fastest, but insects are the most numerous fliers. Migrating swarms sometimes contain billions of insects, taking days to pass by. Birds and bats have wings made from feathers or skin, but insects' wings are made of chitin—the same substance that forms their exoskeleton. Animal flight times vary enormously. Ladybugs touch down after a few minutes, but some sea birds can stay airborne for several years before they land to breed.

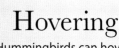

Hovering

Hummingbirds can hover for long periods in still air. Their wings work like propellers, pushing the air downward both when they sweep forward and when they sweep back. The wings of a hummingbird can beat more than 5,000 times a minute, making a humming or buzzing sound. In addition to hovering, hummingbirds can fly sideways or even backward, and they can stop instantly in midair.

Wing sweeping back, pushing air downward

Feathered fliers

With their outstretched legs and necks, greater flamingos look supremely elegant as they cruise through the air. Like most birds, they have lots of special features that enable them to fly. Their skeletons are extra-light, with bones that are hollow or paper-thin, but their wing muscles are huge, making up more than one-third of their body weight. Their lungs are highly efficient, making sure that their muscles get the maximum amount of oxygen. Finally, some feathers keep them warm and streamlined, and others provide the upward lift that keeps them in the air.

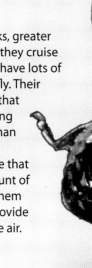

Elytrum fixed in place as soon as ladybug is airborne

Inside a wing

A bird's wing bends at three joints, equivalent to the human shoulder, elbow, and wrist. The power behind a wing beat comes mainly from the pectoral, or breast, muscles. Other muscles adjust the wing's shape in flight, or fold it up.

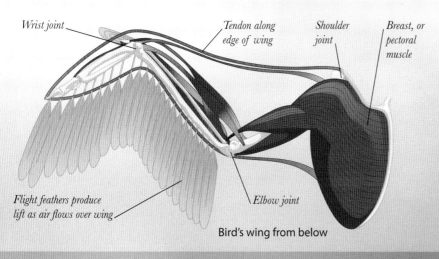

Wrist joint

Tendon along edge of wing

Shoulder joint

Breast, or pectoral muscle

Flight feathers produce lift as air flows over wing

Elbow joint

Bird's wing from below

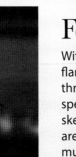

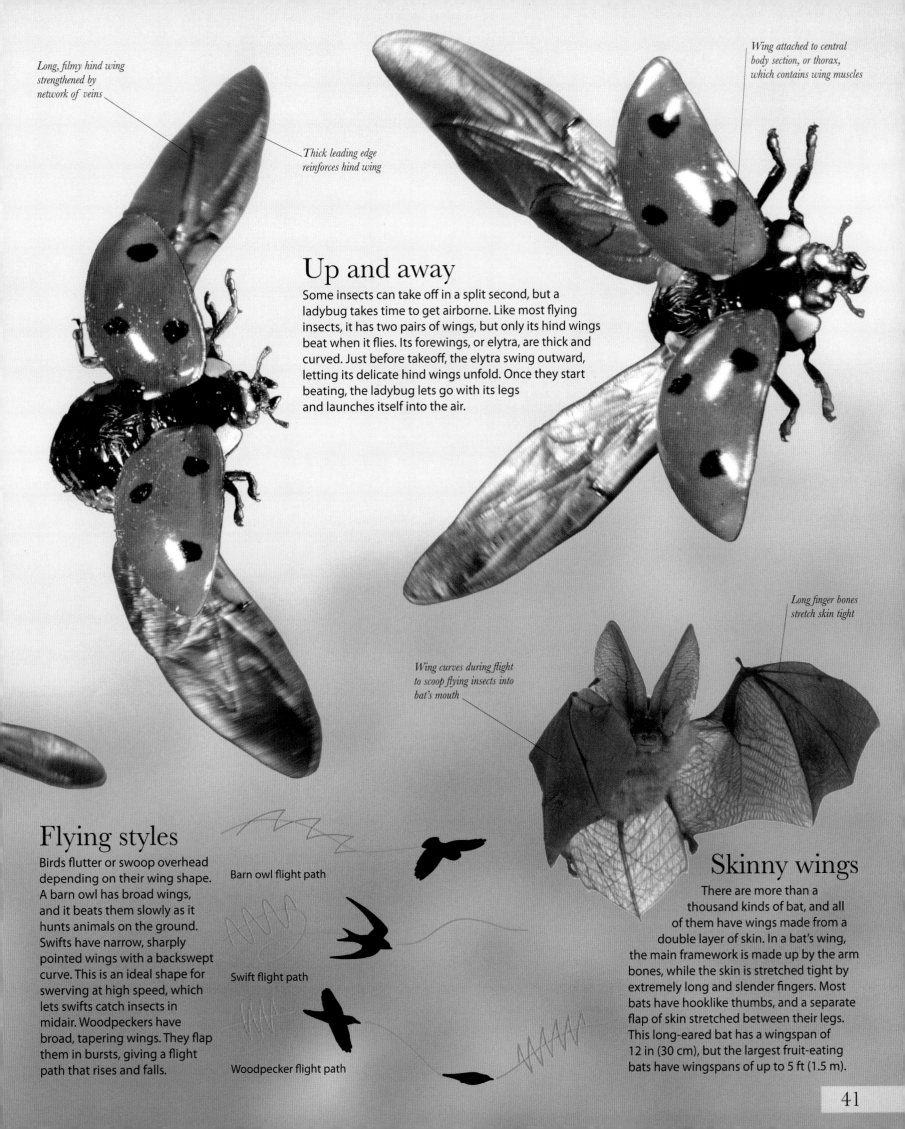

Long, filmy hind wing strengthened by network of veins

Thick leading edge reinforces hind wing

Wing attached to central body section, or thorax, which contains wing muscles

Up and away

Some insects can take off in a split second, but a ladybug takes time to get airborne. Like most flying insects, it has two pairs of wings, but only its hind wings beat when it flies. Its forewings, or elytra, are thick and curved. Just before takeoff, the elytra swing outward, letting its delicate hind wings unfold. Once they start beating, the ladybug lets go with its legs and launches itself into the air.

Long finger bones stretch skin tight

Wing curves during flight to scoop flying insects into bat's mouth

Flying styles

Birds flutter or swoop overhead depending on their wing shape. A barn owl has broad wings, and it beats them slowly as it hunts animals on the ground. Swifts have narrow, sharply pointed wings with a backswept curve. This is an ideal shape for swerving at high speed, which lets swifts catch insects in midair. Woodpeckers have broad, tapering wings. They flap them in bursts, giving a flight path that rises and falls.

Barn owl flight path

Swift flight path

Woodpecker flight path

Skinny wings

There are more than a thousand kinds of bat, and all of them have wings made from a double layer of skin. In a bat's wing, the main framework is made up by the arm bones, while the skin is stretched tight by extremely long and slender fingers. Most bats have hooklike thumbs, and a separate flap of skin stretched between their legs. This long-eared bat has a wingspan of 12 in (30 cm), but the largest fruit-eating bats have wingspans of up to 5 ft (1.5 m).

Swimming and diving

In oceans, rivers, lakes, and ponds, swimming animals are always on the move. To swim, they push against the water, often with flippers or fins. Fast swimmers need to be streamlined, since water is denser than air, but density also helps animals to float. Most swimming animals spend all their lives under water, but many air-breathing animals also dive down from the surface. Whales and seals dive while holding their breath for up to two hours at a time.

Mini swimmers

Ponds are full of miniature animals that swim to find food. These water fleas, or daphnia, swim by flicking their antennae, which look like feathery oars. Daphnia often swim toward the surface after dark to feed on algae and bacteria, and then sink again at dawn. Not much bigger than a pinhead, their top speed is about 0.01 mph (0.02 kph).

Jet-propellers

Trailing its legs behind it, this blue-ringed octopus uses jet propulsion to swim. It sucks water into a cavity in its body and then squirts it backward through a tube called a siphon. The force of the jet pushes the octopus in the opposite direction, making it swim headfirst. This way of swimming is used by other related mollusks, including nautiluses and squid, and also by dragonfly larvae in freshwater.

Diving deep

Elephant seals can move quickly on land, but they are even more impressive under water. They eat squid, octopuses, and deep-sea fish, sometimes diving more than 3,300 ft (1,000 m) to find their food. They can stay under water for up to two hours. Elephant seals manage this incredible feat by storing oxygen in their muscles and blood while they are resting at the surface. They breathe out just before they dive, so their lungs contain only a small amount of air.

Specialized swimming

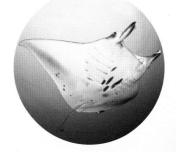

Rays
A ray's broad pectoral fins look like a pair of wings. Rays that are bottom-feeders swim by rippling their fins, but those that live in open water, such as this giant manta ray, usually swim by beating theirs up and down. These rays have the largest "wingspan," which can measure more than 23 ft (7 m) across.

Sea horses
Unlike most fish, seahorses swim with their bodies upright. They push themselves along by fluttering a small fin on their backs and steer by using two tiny fins on either side of their heads. When they are not swimming, they use their tails to hook onto corals and seaweeds.

Eels
Many adult eels, such as this ribbon eel, have a single narrow fin along the length of their bodies. They swim by curving their bodies in the same kind of movement used by swimming snakes. Most eels spend all their lives in water, but some also crawl out and wriggle over land.

Staying up

For fish, staying at the right depth is important for survival. To control this, rays and sharks use their fins, and sharks have an oil-filled liver, which helps to buoy them up. But most fish use a swim bladder to control their buoyancy. The fish can rise or sink by altering the amount of gas in the swim bladder. It takes oxygen from its blood and releases it from a gas gland, blowing the swim bladder up like a balloon.

Swim bladder in center of body, beneath backbone

Dorsal fin keeps fish on course, like a stabilizer

Paired pectoral fins used for steering

Gas gland releases oxygen from blood into swim bladder

Fast fish

With their tapering bodies and scissor-shaped tails, these fusilier fish are built for speed. When they swim, their bodies stay stiff and nearly all the movement comes from their rapidly flicking tails. This way of swimming is also used by some much larger fish that reach record speeds. Over short distances, the fastest fish is the sailfish, which can swim at more than 60 mph (100 kph).

Pectoral fin helps generate lift

Wave peak reaches center of body length

Tail flicks left as wave moves along

Supple swimmers

Most sharks—including this dogfish—move by bending their bodies into curves. As the fish bends, the rear half of its body pushes against the water, with its tail fin adding a final flick. A shark's pectoral fins are slanted upward, which generates lift as it swims. Open-water sharks usually spend all their lives swimming. This keeps water flowing over their gills and helps their blood to circulate.

Head swings right, starting S-shaped wave

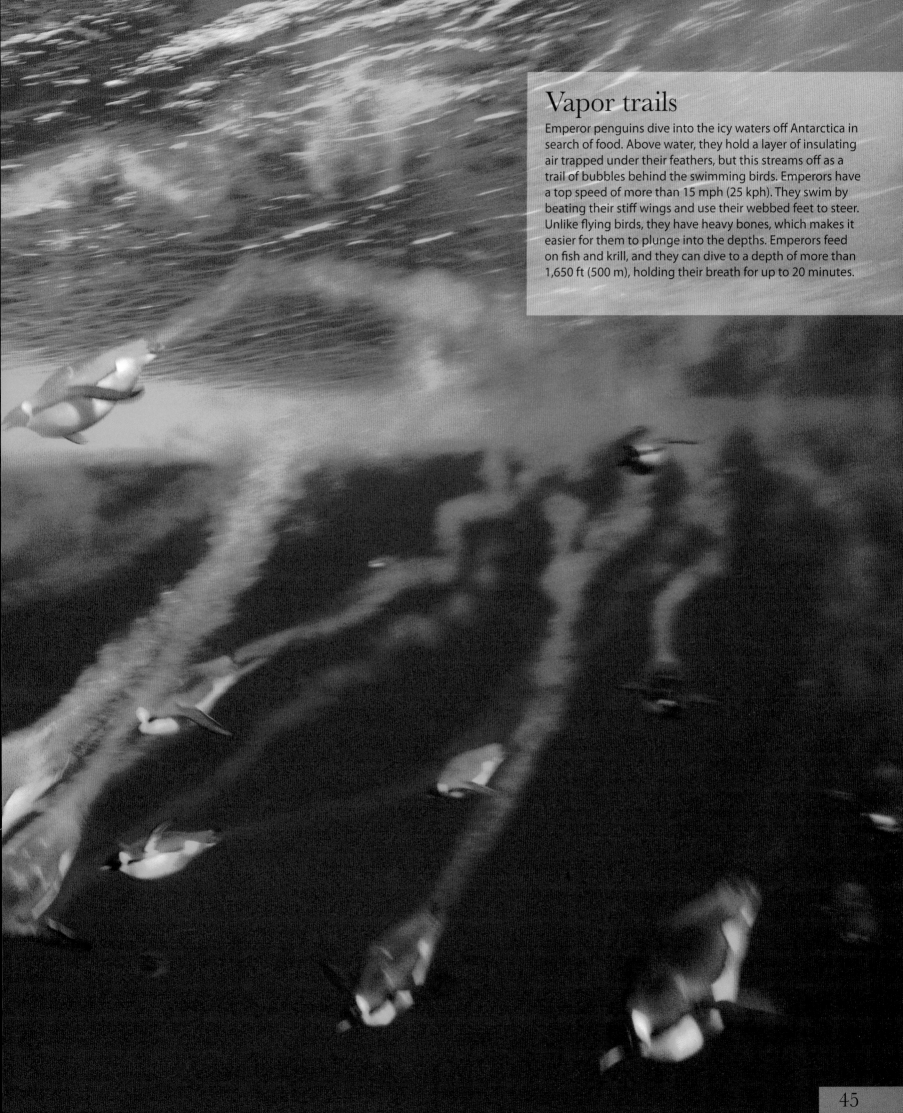

Vapor trails

Emperor penguins dive into the icy waters off Antarctica in search of food. Above water, they hold a layer of insulating air trapped under their feathers, but this streams off as a trail of bubbles behind the swimming birds. Emperors have a top speed of more than 15 mph (25 kph). They swim by beating their stiff wings and use their webbed feet to steer. Unlike flying birds, they have heavy bones, which makes it easier for them to plunge into the depths. Emperors feed on fish and krill, and they can dive to a depth of more than 1,650 ft (500 m), holding their breath for up to 20 minutes.

Borers and burrowers

Life can be dangerous out in the open, and food can be hard to find. Many animals solve these problems by tunneling through their food, or burrowing underground. Using their mouths, feet, or even shells, they eat or scrape their way through their surroundings, staying safely out of sight. Some burrowers, such as naked mole rats, spend their entire lives below ground. Others use their burrows as a base, emerging after dark to feed or to breed.

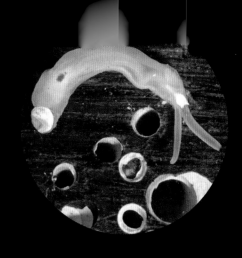

Living drills

Shipworms are clams with sluglike bodies and small, sharp shells. They use their shells like drills to tunnel through submerged wood. In the past, they were a major problem for wooden sailing ships.

How worms burrow

Earthworms may feel smooth and slippery, but they are stronger than they seem. To burrow, an earthworm contracts and relaxes its muscular segments in a set sequence to produce waves of movement down the body. Earthworms usually tunnel near the surface, but in dry weather, they can dig more than 6½ ft (2 m) deep to coil up tight until wetter times return.

Head segments extend as earthworm feeds

Head segments contract and bristles lock in place

Wave of movement passes down body

Tail bristles unlock, tail catches up

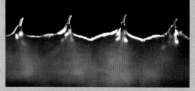

Getting a grip

An earthworm's segments each have four pairs of tiny bristles, or chaetae. When a body segment is contracted, it bulges out, and its bristles lock against the soil. This anchors the segment, so that the worm can push through the ground.

Death in the desert

Predators often strike from above, but Grant's golden mole attacks from below. This one is feeding on a locust, which it has tracked while "swimming" beneath desert sand. The mole picks up on vibrations and can sense the movement of insects and lizards several yards away. Golden moles dig using their front claws, which are like a set of shovels. When the sand is dry, they do not leave tunnels—the sand collapses as soon as they move on.

Extra-thick exoskeleton on head

Armored burrowers

Mole crickets feed on roots and are specially reinforced for burrowing underground. Their heads are armored, and their front legs are short and strong, with clawlike ends highly adept at burrowing and swimming. They spend most of their lives hidden away, but the adults usually have working wings. On summer nights, they leave their burrows and fly off in search of a mate.

Reinforced front leg

Tunnel squad

With their tiny eyes and almost hairless skin, naked mole rats are Africa's strangest burrowing mammals. They feed on the roots of desert plants and dig with their giant incisor teeth. They often tunnel through the insides of nutritious, giant plant roots, or tubers, while keeping the outside layers alive, so they will continue to grow. When naked mole rats dig, they form "chain gangs," with one digging and several more clearing away the soil, passing it back from one to another.

Disappearing trick

Most clams are slow movers, but the razor clam is one of the fastest burrowers in the animal world. It lives on coasts near the low-tide mark, with its slender shell upright in the sand. If in danger, a razor clam can use its powerful foot to dig down to a safe depth of 3 ft (1 m) in under 10 seconds, which is much faster than a human with a shovel.

Life support

Breathing and circulation

Not all animals have lungs, but they all need oxygen. The cells that make up their bodies use oxygen in chemical processes that release energy from food and keep them alive. At the same time, an animal gets rid of carbon dioxide, which its cells produce as waste. For some animals, these two tasks are simple, because gases seep, or diffuse, directly through their skin. But most animals do not work like this. They breathe through lungs or gills, and they use blood to circulate oxygen and nutrients to their cells and to carry away waste. Blood is pumped by the heart. A glass frog's heart weighs less than 0.04 oz (1 g), but a blue whale's can be more than half a ton.

Oxygen from water

Like most animals that live in water, the axolotl draws oxygen out of the water through its gills. Gills are flaps or feathery outgrowths that have a rich blood supply. When water flows over them, oxygen passes into the animal's blood, and carbon dioxide flows out. The axolotl has external gills, which spread out just behind its head. Most fish have internal gills in the cavity behind their mouths. In addition to being used for breathing, gills sometimes double up as filters, helping animals to collect their food.

Thin skin lets oxygen and carbon dioxide spread into and out of the body

Life in a bubble

All spiders get their oxygen from the air, through lungs on their undersides. These lungs are called book lungs, because they are made up of tiny flaps like the pages of a book. But one spider, the water spider, spends most of its life beneath the surface of ponds. It makes an air-filled "diving bell," which it holds under water with a net of silk. When the spider hunts, it carries a slim film of air, which works like an aqualung, on the rear of its body, or abdomen.

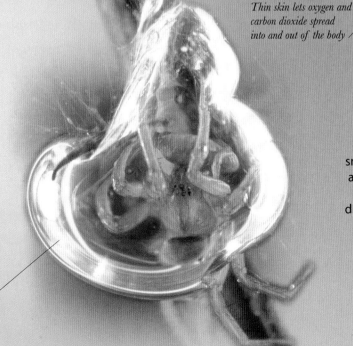

Air collected by the spider on frequent visits to the pond surface

Bodies that breathe

Like shadowy ghosts, sea butterflies swim through the oceans using transparent flaps that look like wings. These tiny mollusks are snails, but they do not have shells, and they get all the oxygen they need without gills or lungs. Because their bodies are flat and thin, oxygen diffuses into them from the water, while carbon dioxide diffuses out. This way of exchanging gases is used by many small animals that live in water and also by earthworms on land.

Breathing with lungs

On a cold winter's day, a red deer produces a cloud of mist as it roars to rival males. Like all mammals, it breathes with a pair of lungs, which are hollow spaces on either side of the heart. To breathe in, it uses muscles that expand its chest, sucking in fresh air. When the breathing muscles relax, the air moves back out. To roar, the deer takes an extra-large breath and then forces it through its throat.

One-way traffic

When mammals breathe, air travels into their lungs and then back out again. A bird's lungs are much better at collecting oxygen, because air flows straight through them, instead of in and out. Air sacs connected to the lungs keep the air on the move. Thanks to this super-efficient system, birds can breathe high in the sky, where the air is very thin.

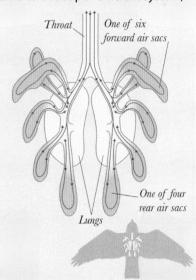

Throat
One of six forward air sacs
Lungs
One of four rear air sacs

Air flow
When a bird breathes in, oxygen-rich air (shown in red) moves into its rear air sacs. After flowing through the lungs, stale air (shown in blue) moves into the forward air sacs, before being breathed out.

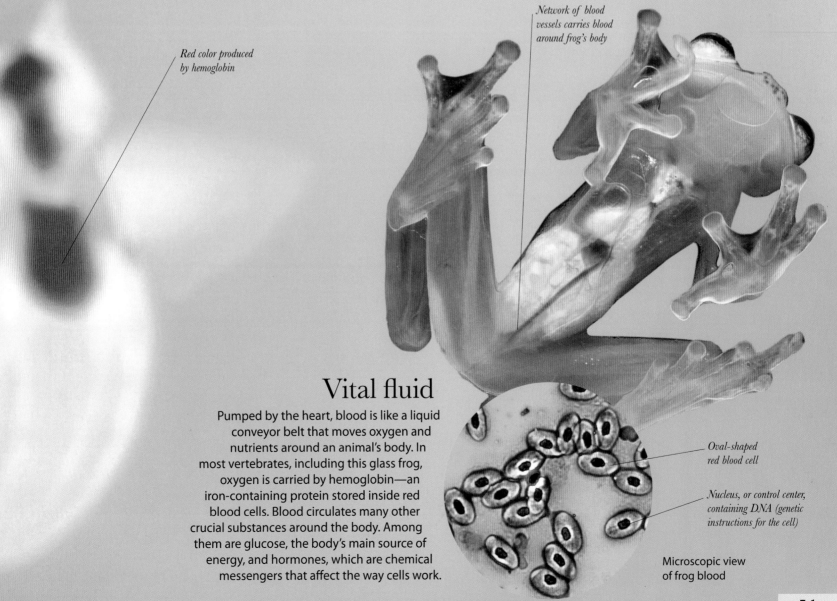

Red color produced by hemoglobin

Network of blood vessels carries blood around frog's body

Oval-shaped red blood cell

Nucleus, or control center, containing DNA (genetic instructions for the cell)

Microscopic view of frog blood

Vital fluid

Pumped by the heart, blood is like a liquid conveyor belt that moves oxygen and nutrients around an animal's body. In most vertebrates, including this glass frog, oxygen is carried by hemoglobin—an iron-containing protein stored inside red blood cells. Blood circulates many other crucial substances around the body. Among them are glucose, the body's main source of energy, and hormones, which are chemical messengers that affect the way cells work.

Crowning glory

Creeping over rocks off the coast of Borneo, a sea slug, or nudibranch, shows off its stunning color scheme. It has two yellow horns, or rhinophores, which sense food by smell, but its most eye-catching feature is a tuft of feathery gills. Spreading out in the water, these thin flaps collect oxygen, letting it pass into the sea slug's blood. Sea slugs have very poor eyesight and cannot see their amazing colors themselves. Instead, they use them as a warning to other animals, showing that they are not good to eat.

Nerves and brains

Nerves play an essential part in making animal bodies work. Using tiny electrical pulses, they make muscles contract, enabling movement. They also carry information from sense organs so that animals can react to the world around them. Nerves do this by passing on signals. Simple animals, such as jellyfish, have a mesh of nerve cells throughout their bodies. But in most animals, the nervous system has major highways called nerves and nerve cords, which connect with the brain. In the brain, information is processed and stored, letting animals behave in amazingly complex ways.

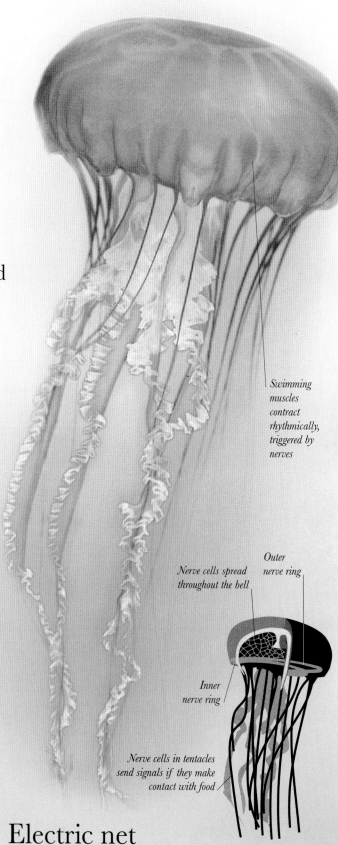

Swimming muscles contract rhythmically, triggered by nerves

Changing brain

A fox's brain contains more than 100 billion nerve cells, or neurons. Unlike most cells in a fox's body, the neurons are in place when a cub is born. From its very first day, the cub can perform instinctive behavior such as feeding on milk, because this action is programmed into its brain. As the fox grows up, it learns many new kinds of behavior, including how to hunt. As the fox learns new skills and absorbs fresh information, new connections are made between the neurons in its brain.

Nerve cells spread throughout the bell

Outer nerve ring

Inner nerve ring

Nerve cells in tentacles send signals if they make contact with food

Nerve cells

Nerves are made up of nerve cells, or neurons, which are much thinner than a hair, but in large animals, they can be many yards long. They have a main thread, or axon, and many fine strands called dendrites. These connect to other neurons and sensory cells by chemical junctions called synapses. If a synapse is triggered, the neuron fires, and an electrical signal flashes down the cell.

Dendrite connects with another cell

Nucleus

Signals speed along axon toward terminal fibers

Axon

Sheath of myelin surrounds axon

Cell body

Terminal fiber links to other neurons

Superfast neuron
In vertebrates, many neurons are insulated by a fatty substance called myelin. This lets them carry signals at more than 185 mph (300 kph)—much faster than the neurons in other animals.

Electric net

Jellyfish and their relatives have a pattern of nerve cells spread throughout their bodies like a net. Like all nerves, they are connected by synapses, which let signals jump from one nerve cell to the next. Some jellyfish also have a ring of nerves on the inner and outer edges of their bell. The outer ring coordinates the jellyfish's sense of touch, while the inner ring controls swimming, by making the muscles in its bell contract together.

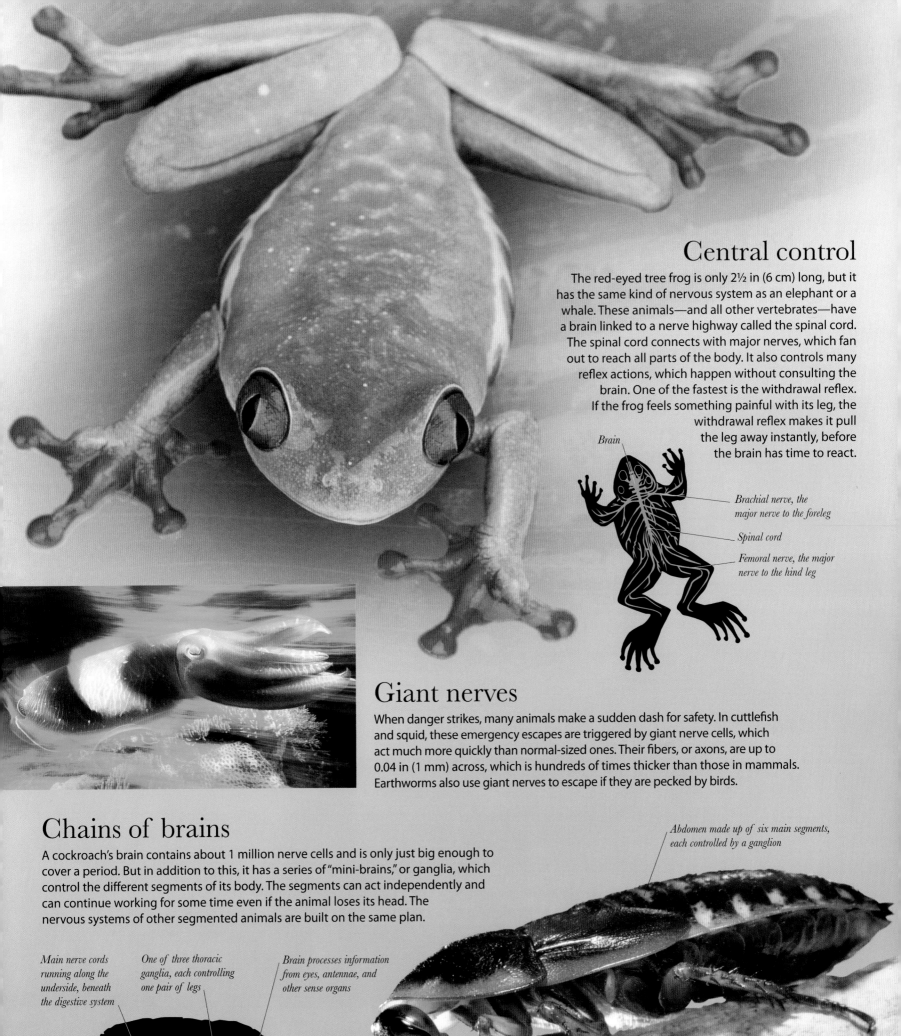

Central control

The red-eyed tree frog is only 2½ in (6 cm) long, but it has the same kind of nervous system as an elephant or a whale. These animals—and all other vertebrates—have a brain linked to a nerve highway called the spinal cord. The spinal cord connects with major nerves, which fan out to reach all parts of the body. It also controls many reflex actions, which happen without consulting the brain. One of the fastest is the withdrawal reflex. If the frog feels something painful with its leg, the withdrawal reflex makes it pull the leg away instantly, before the brain has time to react.

Brain

Brachial nerve, the major nerve to the foreleg

Spinal cord

Femoral nerve, the major nerve to the hind leg

Giant nerves

When danger strikes, many animals make a sudden dash for safety. In cuttlefish and squid, these emergency escapes are triggered by giant nerve cells, which act much more quickly than normal-sized ones. Their fibers, or axons, are up to 0.04 in (1 mm) across, which is hundreds of times thicker than those in mammals. Earthworms also use giant nerves to escape if they are pecked by birds.

Chains of brains

A cockroach's brain contains about 1 million nerve cells and is only just big enough to cover a period. But in addition to this, it has a series of "mini-brains," or ganglia, which control the different segments of its body. The segments can act independently and can continue working for some time even if the animal loses its head. The nervous systems of other segmented animals are built on the same plan.

Abdomen made up of six main segments, each controlled by a ganglion

Main nerve cords running along the underside, beneath the digestive system

One of three thoracic ganglia, each controlling one pair of legs

Brain processes information from eyes, antennae, and other sense organs

Temperature control

On the shores of Antarctica, winter temperatures can drop to −40°F (−40°C), and storm-force winds make it feel colder still. Despite this, penguins keep their bodies at 100°F (38°C)—the same temperature as birds in the jungle. Like all birds and mammals, they are warm-blooded, or endothermic. Their muscles and livers keep them warm by acting like chemical furnaces, fueled by energy from food. Most other animals are cold-blooded, or ectothermic. Instead of generating their warmth internally, they get it from outside. In some habitats, such as the deep sea, cold-blooded animals are always cold. But in warm places, they sometimes get too hot and have to seek shelter in the shade.

Soaking up sunshine

Lizards move slowly when they are cold, so they need a kick-start of warmth before they can start to hunt. By basking in the morning sunshine, a lizard can raise its body temperature to 86°F (30°C), even when the air is still cool. As the day heats up, the lizard keeps its temperature steady by moving in and out of the shade. At sunset, it crawls into a safe crevice, where its body cools down for the night.

Ocellated lizard

Well padded

Stretched out on a beach, a male elephant seal seems to slump over the sand. Its oversized outline is produced by a thick jacket of body fat, or blubber, which keeps it warm when it dives. Blubber is poor at conducting heat, so it stops the seal's warmth from ebbing away into the cold water outside. On land, this layer of fat can easily make the seal overheat. To prevent this from happening, the seal's body automatically diverts blood into its skin, letting surplus heat escape into the air.

Cooling off

In warm weather, kangaroos lounge under trees or rocks, where they are shaded from the sun. But if the air is hot, they use an emergency cooling system. They lick their forearms until the fur is wet. The saliva then evaporates, and the evaporation sucks heat from blood flowing through the arms. Many other mammals use evaporation to keep cool. Dogs and foxes cool down by panting, while horses and large antelopes sweat, just like humans do. Many birds pant by fluttering their throats, but some have a stranger way of losing heat: they squirt liquid droppings onto their legs.

Shivering snakes

Snakes are cold-blooded, but this diamond python has an unusual way of warming up its eggs. By shivering its muscles, it generates heat, which keeps the eggs up to 9°F (5°C) warmer than the surrounding air. Snakes are not the only cold-blooded animals that shiver. In cold habitats, some moths and bumblebees warm up by shivering before they fly.

Superfast fish

Most fish are cold-blooded, so their temperature is the same as the water around them. Tuna and swordfish are an exception—their central swimming muscles stay warm, letting them speed continuously through the seas. These muscles have a dark color and a special blood supply. Warm blood flowing out of the muscles meets cold blood flowing in, and transfers most of its heat. This system—called a countercurrent—stops warmth from escaping from the muscles.

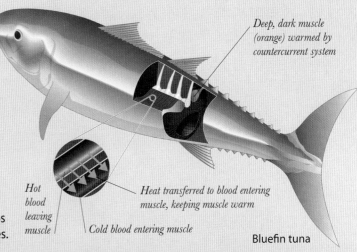

Deep, dark muscle (orange) warmed by countercurrent system

Hot blood leaving muscle

Heat transferred to blood entering muscle, keeping muscle warm

Cold blood entering muscle

Bluefin tuna

Group hug

Watched over by a pair of adults, emperor penguin chicks huddle together on the ice. They are insulated by body fat and by their soft gray down, but huddling gives them an extra way of staying warm. These huddles, or crèches, can contain thousands of young birds. The chicks keep their heads down, out of the wind, and they keep shuffling toward the center of the crèche, so that each one gets its share of the warmth. When the chicks are five months old, they start to grow their adult plumage. The crèches break up, and the young penguins head off for the sea.

Adult emperor penguin watches over crèche

Keeping clean

For most animals, cleaning is part of life's routine. It keeps their bodies in good condition and can get rid of troublesome parasites. Mammals and birds clean their fur and feathers, and even animals as small as houseflies carefully clean their wings. In addition to scraping away dirt, animals often spread out waxes and oils, which act as waterproofing. Cleaning is a personal business, and most animals clean only themselves, or others of their own kind. But the animal world includes species, such as some birds, fish, and shrimp, that make a living from this kind of work. They pick over their "clients," eating anything edible that they find.

Well groomed

Like all cats, a tiger grooms its fur with its tongue and teeth. Its tongue has rough, backward-pointing barbs that work like a comb, pulling out any loose hairs. It removes large objects—such as hooked seeds—with the incisor teeth at the front of its jaws.

Food on the move

In the ocean off Hawaii, this green turtle has attracted a mixed group of surgeonfish. The fish are scraping algae and encrusting animals from its body surface. By cleaning the shell, they help to keep the turtle streamlined. Surgeonfish are only part-time cleaners, but some fish and shrimp get all their food in this way. On coral reefs, they set up feeding stations in prominent places, and their customers often line up to be cleaned.

A surgeonfish's small mouth has a row of narrow teeth that scrapes food off the turtle's body surface

Dirty habits

Good hygiene usually helps animals to stay healthy, but for some, habits that seem dirty to us can actually help in the fight for survival. Many mammals wallow in mud or leave messages by spreading their urine. Sloths hide in the treetops by letting algae grow in their fur.

Grubby coat
Unlike most mammals, the sloth does not groom its fur. Microscopic algae grow on the hairs, giving its coat a greenish tinge and a moldy smell.

Sticky messages
Bushbabies, or galagos, live and feed in trees. They wash their hands and feet with urine either to mark their territories or to improve their grip.

Mud bath
The warthog does not have sweat glands, so it cools down by wallowing in mud. Mud also helps to protect it from bloodsucking flies.

You scratch my back...

For chimps, grooming is an important social activity involving all the members of a troop. Chimps groom each other to maintain bonds and to defuse tension after a dispute. In a troop, the smartest, strongest, or most forceful chimps earn a high rank, or importance, in chimp society. Low-ranking chimps groom others the most, while dominant ones spend a lot of time being groomed, but often do not groom the others.

Preen clean

Feathers need constant care, and birds can spend hours a day maintaining them by preening. This Japanese crane uses it beak like a precision instrument, nibbling its feathers so that they lie flat. At the same time, it removes lice and other parasites and covers the feathers with a waxy substance from its preen gland. Many birds wash in water before they preen, but some ground-dwelling kinds—including chickens and grouse—keep their feathers dry and bathe in dust instead.

Ticklish moment

Like a feathered mountaineer, a yellow-billed oxpecker clings to the neck of a giraffe. This African bird spends most of its life aboard large mammals, where it hunts for ticks and other parasites using a beak that is flat like a pair of shears. Oxpeckers help their hosts by getting rid of pests, but they also peck at wounds, which makes it harder for them to heal.

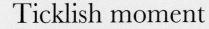

Earwax can provide extra food for oxpeckers

Oxpecker braces itself with its tail

Crane's bill probes beneath its feathers to get oil from the preen gland—a swelling at the base of its tail

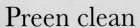

Young feather louse

Dust storm

It is more than ¾ in (2 cm) thick, but an elephant's tough hide needs just as much care as our own soft skin. This young African elephant is enjoying a dust bath, coating its gray-black skin with pale-brown dry soil, or dust. The dust that settles on its skin absorbs grease and smothers skin parasites, such as ticks, lice, or flies. It also helps to screen the elephant's skin from the harsh rays of the Sun. Elephants also bathe in water and mud, and they rarely pass up the opportunity to scratch their skin on a tree trunk or rock face.

Animal rhythms

The world is full of repeating changes, or rhythms, that affect animals' lives. They include the 24-hour rhythm of day and night, the year-long rhythm of the seasons, and the rhythm of the tides. All over the world, animals keep in step with these changes, so that they can feed and breed when conditions are best. Animals do not have calendars, and they cannot plan ahead. They stay in step by sensing changes around them and by using built-in body clocks, which are kept ticking by hormones and by nerves.

Breeding with the tides

The rhythm of the tides, controlled by the motion of the Sun and the Moon, dominates seashore life and even affects animals far out to sea. The time between high tides is normally 12.5 hours, but extra-large "spring" tides occur every two weeks. Slender fish called California grunions use these tides to breed. When the spring tide is at its height, they wriggle their way onto beaches, where they mate and lay their eggs. A month later, during another spring tide, the eggs hatch, and the young grunions are swept out to sea.

Mass awakening

In North America, red-sided garter snakes hibernate together in burrows and crevices underground. When spring brings warmth and plentiful food, it is time to breed. The males emerge first. When a female appears, up to 100 males fight to be her partner, forming a writhing mass called a mating ball. The timing of this amorous frenzy varies according to the local climate. In the southern US, garter snakes can mate as early as February, but in Canada's cold climate, they may not emerge until June.

Split shifts

Very few animals stay active around the clock. Instead, most are either active by day (diurnal) or active by night (nocturnal). By waking at different times, diurnal and nocturnal animals can live in similar ways without competing head-on for food. For example, butterflies and moths both feed at flowers, but butterflies come out during the day, while most moths are active after dark.
In the same way, raptors, or birds of prey, hunt by day—at night, they are replaced by owls.

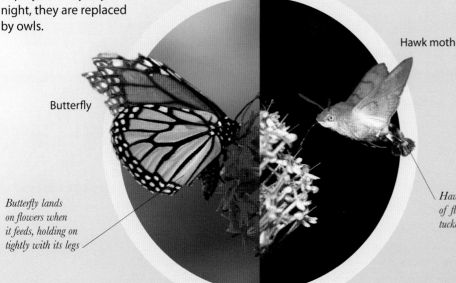

Hawk moth

Butterfly

Butterfly lands on flowers when it feeds, holding on tightly with its legs

Hawk moth hovers in front of flowers, keeping its legs tucked up against its body

Feeding with the tides

For sanderlings and many other waders, the rise and fall of the tide is much more important than the rhythm of night and day. When the tide is low, sanderlings scuttle along the water's edge, snapping up small animals that are exposed by the waves. At high tide, they stop feeding and rest until the tide turns once more. Waders have very sensitive bills, and they often feed by moonlight when the tide is going out.

Outer covering, or exoskeleton, is shed for a final time before cicada mates and lays eggs

Population cycles

Animal numbers often change from year to year. These changes are caused by many factors, including the weather and food supply. Usually, they are impossible to predict, but in some animals, they rise and fall in cycles that last a set number of years.

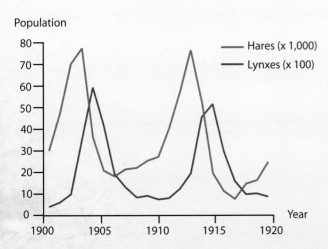

Population

— Hares (x 1,000)
— Lynxes (x 100)

Canadian lynx with snowshoe hare prey

Boom and bust

In the Arctic, the numbers of snowshoe hares and Canadian lynxes soar and then crash every nine or 10 years. The crashes are triggered when the hares start to run short of food. The lynx population drops a year or two later, when they start to run out of hares to eat.

Years in the making

North American periodical cicadas have some of the longest rhythms in the animal world. There are several species, and each one has a life cycle lasting exactly 13 or 17 years. The cicadas spend most of their lives underground, sucking sap from roots, but after 13 or 17 years, they crawl up tree trunks, all at once, to mate and lay their eggs. For a few weeks, the air is filled with ear-piercing sounds, as billions of cicadas call to each other among the trees. After breeding, the adults die, and another 13 or 17 years pass before the next brood emerges from the ground.

Migration

Every year, migrating animals take part in immense journeys over land, in the air, and through the oceans. Guided partly by instinct, they arrive at their breeding grounds when the food supply reaches its peak. After raising their young, they head off to their nonbreeding range, where they spend the rest of the year. Some migrant birds can travel more than 30,000 miles (50,000 km) each year. The prospect of extra food and space makes these hard, dangerous journeys worthwhile.

Head contains magnetite, possibly helping the migrant bird sense Earth's magnetic field, like a compass does

Animals on the move

Arctic terns make a round-trip journey between the Arctic and the Antarctic, traveling at least 20,000 miles (32,000 km) a year. Gray whales travel 12,500 miles (20,000 km)—farther than any other mammal. Monarch butterflies travel up to 3,000 miles (4,800 km).

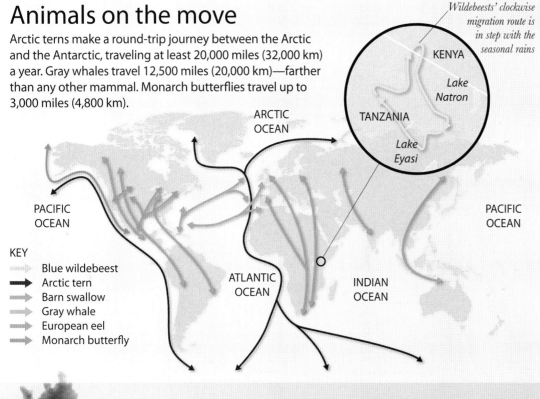

Wildebeests' clockwise migration route is in step with the seasonal rains

ARCTIC OCEAN

KENYA

Lake Natron

TANZANIA

Lake Eyasi

PACIFIC OCEAN

PACIFIC OCEAN

ATLANTIC OCEAN

INDIAN OCEAN

KEY

- Blue wildebeest
- Arctic tern
- Barn swallow
- Gray whale
- European eel
- Monarch butterfly

Finding the way

Snow geese migrate between the Arctic, where they nest, and the southern United States, where they winter. Like many migrants, their journeys are triggered by the changing length of the days as summer gives way to fall, and as winter gives way to spring. Once they are airborne, they use a range of cues to find their way. These include landmarks, such as coasts and the position of the stars. They even have an internal compass that senses the direction of Earth's magnetic field.

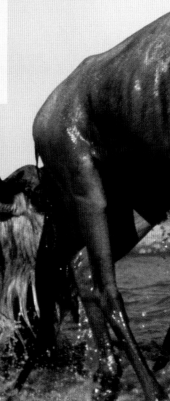

Mini migrations

On Christmas Island in the Indian Ocean, millions of red land crabs emerge from the forest during the annual monsoon rains. They head for the coast, where they mate and shed their eggs into the sea. The journey to the coast takes them about a week. When they have finished breeding, they head back to their homes on the forest floor.

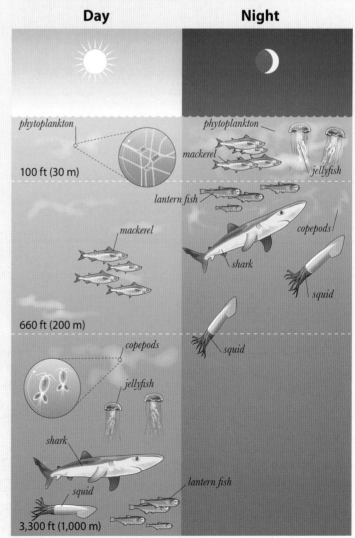

Trip of a lifetime

Long-lived animals, such as whales, may migrate dozens of times in their lives. But for some animals, migration is a once-in-a-lifetime experience. Monarch butterflies usually migrate just once and so do sockeye salmon. After battling their way upriver and spawning, the exhausted adults die.

Daily commute

During the day, tiny animals called copepods hide in the darkness of the deep ocean. But when night falls, clouds of them migrate upward to eat phytoplankton (microscopic algae at the surface. The copepods' predators follow them.

Danger time

In East Africa, wildebeest migrate in gigantic herds that snake their way across grassy plains. Hunger keeps them on the move, and it also attracts a variety of predators, including lions, hyenas, and crocodiles. These wildebeest are crossing the muddy waters of the Mara River, where crocodiles kill hundreds of wildebeest every year.

Day   **Night**

phytoplankton

phytoplankton

mackerel

100 ft (30 m)

jellyfish

lantern fish

mackerel

shark

copepods

squid

660 ft (200 m)

squid

copepods

jellyfish

shark

squid

lantern fish

3,300 ft (1,000 m)

Surviving extremes

Some animals thrive in almost unbelievable extremes. In volcanic vents on the seabed, Pompeii worms endure water temperatures of up to 176°F (80°C), while in the Arctic, wood frogs and insects survive being frozen solid for several months each year. In the highest mountains, birds routinely feed at heights of 26,000 ft (8,000 m), where a human would be left gasping for breath. In many habitats, every year brings its share of heat, cold, or drought, and animals often survive by shutting down when life gets tough. When conditions improve, they become active once more.

Heat freak

Scientists discovered Pompeii worms in the 1980s when exploring superhot volcanic vents on the Pacific Ocean floor. The vent water can reach 750°F (400°C), but the worms live in a narrow "comfort zone," between the vents and the surrounding cold ocean. They keep their heads in cold water, while their tails take the heat.

Hibernation

In winter, cold weather often makes food hard to find. Many mammals, including the common dormouse, survive by going into hibernation. True hibernation is very different from sleep. When an animal hibernates, its body temperature drops to a very low level, and its heart beats only a few times each minute. It gets its energy from reserves of body fat, which it stores up before hibernation starts.

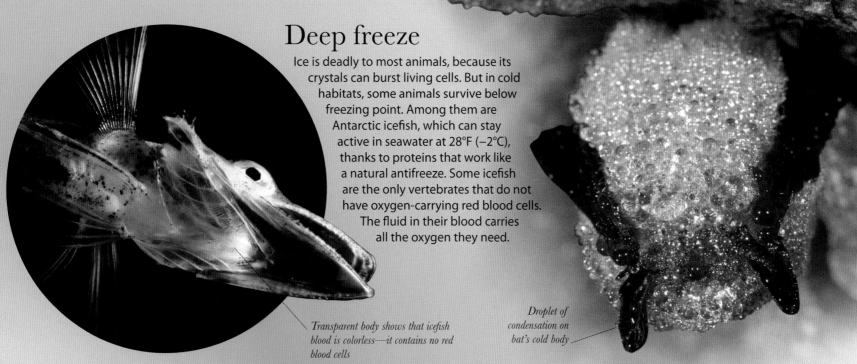

Deep freeze

Ice is deadly to most animals, because its crystals can burst living cells. But in cold habitats, some animals survive below freezing point. Among them are Antarctic icefish, which can stay active in seawater at 28°F (–2°C), thanks to proteins that work like a natural antifreeze. Some icefish are the only vertebrates that do not have oxygen-carrying red blood cells. The fluid in their blood carries all the oxygen they need.

Transparent body shows that icefish blood is colorless—it contains no red blood cells

Droplet of condensation on bat's cold body

Chilling out

Deep in a cave, a hibernating whiskered bat waits for winter to come to an end. Its body temperature is just a few degrees above freezing, and droplets of water have condensed on its fur. During winter, the bat wakes up for short periods and shivers, which helps to keep its muscles functioning normally.

Hazelnut stored by dormouse for eating when it wakes briefly from hibernation

Leg rest

Microscopic animals can be amazingly good at coping with extreme conditions. Tardigrades stow their legs away if conditions turn dry. Once they have done this, they show no signs of life. They can remain sealed up for 10 years or more.

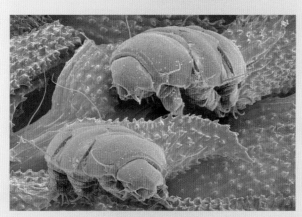

Active tardigrades with legs extended

Skin cocoon peels away as frog emerges

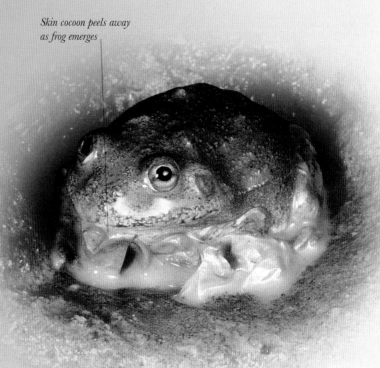

Waxy covering produced by tardigrade prevents water loss when dormant

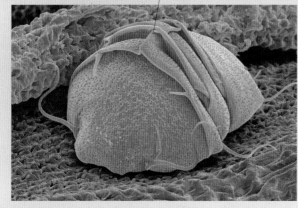

Dormant tardigrade with legs retracted

Waiting for rain

In Australia, the water-holding frog survives in deserts by holing up underground. It stores water in its bladder and seals itself in a cocoon of dead, moisture-retaining skin. After heavy storms, it digs its way to the surface, where it lays its eggs in temporary pools. The pools soon dry, but by then, the frogs and froglets are safely hidden away.

Animal diets

Fuel for living

All animals need energy to live and they get it by eating food. Many feed on leaves, fruit, and seeds. Others eat other animals or dead remains. Some animals can survive for weeks between meals, but most need to find food every day. Food energy is processed by living things in a food chain, which begins when plants make food from sunlight. This energy is passed on when animals feed on the plants.

Wing muscles powered by food energy

Feeding tools

Meat-eaters and plant-eaters have varied equipment for gathering and breaking down their food. Mammals, for instance, have differently shaped teeth depending on their diet. Lions have pointed canine teeth that grip their prey, and scissorlike carnassial teeth that slice up meat. In contrast, rabbits have continually growing incisor teeth that gnaw grass and rows of molar teeth that grind up plant matter at the backs of their jaws.

Lion skull

Carnassial tooth has jagged, slicing edge

Canine tooth has sharp point

Sharp incisor tooth has flat, snipping edge

Berry banquet

Fieldfares feast on berries during winter months, when other food can be hard to find. This harvest is created from sunlight, which trees collect with their leaves through a process called photosynthesis. Like all plants, trees use this solar energy to grow and to make energy-rich substances, including sugars and starch. Fieldfares and other fruit-eaters eat this food, and, in return, they help to scatter a tree's seeds.

Flat molar tooth has raised, grinding ridges

Rabbit skull

Food chain

Solar energy
The Sun supplies energy to most living things. Plants use sunlight to make food, which is then passed along the food chain as chemical energy when animals eat the plants or each other.

Grass
In the vast praries of North America, sunlight is collected by grasses and other plants. Grasses use solar energy to grow leaves and seeds, as well as a dense network of roots.

Grasshopper
The prairies teem with grasshoppers and other plant-eating insects. Their numbers explode in summer when plants are growing fast, creating a huge supply of food.

Leopard frog
At night, the leopard frog emerges from pools to hunt. Its diet includes grasshoppers, as well as many other small prairie animals, from earthworms to centipedes.

Garter snake
This slender snake lives in a wide variety of habitats, particularly in areas where it is damp. The garter snake hunts and catches leopard frogs on land or swims after them in water.

Harrier
Sweeping low over the prairies, the northern harrier snatches up snakes in its talons. This hawk is a top predator, meaning that it has no natural enemies.

Multipurpose beak can deal with insects and worms, as well as fruit

Sharp mouthparts fold away under aphid's body when not in use

Berry packed with energy-rich sugars made during summer months

Fluid food

Some plant foods are tough to eat and even harder to digest. However, plants also produce sugary liquids that are eaten by many animals, including insects and birds. One of these fluids is nectar, which plants make in their flowers, and another is sap, which travels through their stems. Aphids specialize in eating sap. They stab the stems with their hollow mouthparts and drink the sap as it oozes out from the plant.

Worker ant carries a piece of leaf back to nest

Meat feast

Wrapping its coils around a gecko, this paradise tree snake waits for its venom to work before starting on its meal. Like many predators, the snake uses stealth to track down its prey and strikes before its victim has a chance to escape. Hunting takes time, and it can be dangerous work, but successful predators reap the benefits. Meat is packed full of energy and nutrients, so meat-eaters need fewer meals than plant-eaters to keep themselves well fed.

Constant gardeners

Animals don't always feed directly on the food they gather. Leafcutter ants carry pieces of leaf down from the treetops into their nests underground. Here, the ants use the leaves to make compost gardens, where they cultivate a special fungus. The ant colony feeds on the fungus and makes sure that it has the right conditions to grow. When a queen ant flies off to start a new nest, she carries some of the fungus food with her.

Open-air pantry

Using its hook-tipped beak, a male red-backed shrike impales a beetle on a thorn. The bird has already caught and spiked a lizard and a butterfly, and it will make more pantries when this one is full. When prey is easy to find, the shrike stores away its excess supplies in heathland trees or bushes and then returns to feed if food becomes scarce. Food storage is unusual among hunters, because dead prey is difficult to keep fresh. The shrike's storage system dries out the insects and small animals quickly, making them safe to eat over a period of time.

Grazing and browsing

Vast grasslands cover one-fifth of Earth's land surface. They are home to grazers, including many of the world's largest mammals, which fuel their bodies on a diet of pure grass. Although grasses grow in abundance, they are low in energy and nutrients, and they are difficult to digest. To survive, grazers spend much of the day feeding. Browsing animals are selective feeders and they gather the leaves, buds, fruit, or seeds of particular plants to eat.

Prairie giant

The American bison is a heavyweight grazer with a big appetite—adult males need to consume up to 110 lb (50 kg) of grass a day. Like many other large grazing mammals, the bison is a ruminant with a special digestive system for breaking down its tough, fibrous food. At one time, giant herds of more than a million bison roamed the North American prairies. Today, however, their numbers have shrunk dramatically, due to overhunting and to people plowing up too much of the grasslands to grow crops.

Long, curved claws clamp limbs to branches, letting sloth climb or hang without tiring

Geese store body fat, converted from grass in their diet

Grazing geese

Mammals are not the only large animals that feed by grazing. These pink-footed geese are eating grass during a migration stopover near England's east coast. Although they swim well and have webbed feet, geese gather most of their food on land. The birds have no teeth, but they can tear up grass by gripping clumps in their beaks and then giving them a sharp tug.

Digesting plant food

Ruminant mammals, such as sheep and cattle, cannot digest the tough substance in grass called cellulose. They get help from microorganisms, which live in the rumen—the largest of their four stomach chambers. Here, the microorganisms break down the cellulose, and the animal then regurgitates its food to chew it for a second time. The food then travels through the other stomach chambers, where its nutrients are absorbed.

Slow-motion meal

Clinging tightly to a branch with its hook-shaped claws, a two-toed sloth leisurely chews its way through a leaf. Sloths spend almost all of their time in trees and are legendary for their unhurried movements, spending many hours resting each day. A sloth digests its food equally slowly. It can take more than a month for leaves to pass through its body—a record digestion time for any plant-eating mammal.

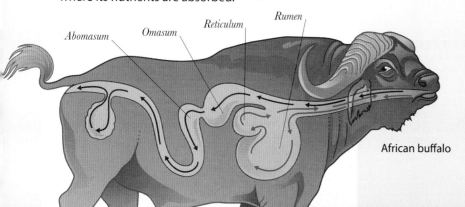

Abomasum Omasum Reticulum Rumen

African buffalo

Sloths feed only on leaves from a small variety of trees

Fur forms peaks, helping rainwater run off body during feeding

Extended wrist bone closes against panda's true thumb when it is holding stems

Underwater pasture

Marine iguanas from the Galápagos Islands are some of the world's strangest plant-eating animals. Instead of feeding on the shore, they dive into the sea to graze on underwater seaweed beds. The iguanas use their rudderlike tails for swimming and resist the pull of the water by clinging to rocks with their sharp claws. Although the Galápagos Islands lie on the equator, the sea around them is cold. After grazing, marine iguanas return to land and bask in the sunshine. This raises their body temperature and helps them to digest their food.

Bamboo feasting

The giant panda is a bear that has taken up a vegetarian diet. Uniquely for a bear, it feeds almost entirely on bamboo, even though it still has the teeth of a meat-eater. The panda's flat paws have a specially extended wrist bone that works like a movable, or opposable, thumb, and grips bamboo stems. Compared to other plant-eaters, the panda is not very efficient at digesting its food, and so it must eat up to 90 lb (40 kg) of bamboo a day.

Feeding at flowers

There are more than 250,000 different kinds of flowering plant, and more than three-quarters of them produce nectar, an energy-rich liquid that animals feed on. In return, animals pollinate the flowers by spreading grains of pollen from flower to flower, so that seeds can form. Flower-feeders include huge numbers of insects and some specialized birds and mammals. In addition to nectar, some animals eat pollen, or even flowers themselves.

Beak closed when feeding, except for small gap at tip

Night flights

As night falls, daytime pollinators disappear, and different animals set off to visit flowers. These Mexican long-tongued bats are feeding at the flowers of a century plant, which grow in clusters on the end of long stalks. Unlike insect-eating bats, those that visit flowers have good eyesight and a keen sense of smell. To a human nose, bat-pollinated flowers often smell sickly sweet, but their aroma can attract bats from more than half a mile (1 km) downwind.

Food on the wing

Beating its wings more than 50 times a second, a hummingbird stays rock-steady as it feeds at a columbine flower. Its beak reaches deep into the bloom, while its tongue darts in and out to lap up nectar. Despite being just 4 in (10 cm) long, the ruby-throated hummingbird migrates from Central America as far north as Canada, fueling up with nectar before starting its flight.

Rapidly beating wings keep hummingbird directly beneath flower

Part-time visitors

Using its jaws, a leaf beetle scrapes pollen from the male parts, or stamens, of a flower. It eats most of the pollen grains, but some stick to its body, ready to be transferred to the next flower that it visits. Leaf beetles get only part of their food from flowers. They visit flowers where there is room to clamber around and the pollen or nectar is easy to reach. The rest of their diet comes from eating other parts of the plant, such as the leaves and seeds.

Strong, leathery flowers resist damage caused by feeding bats

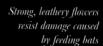

Agile climbers

Australia is home to some acrobatic marsupials that visit flowers in bushes and trees. This pygmy possum feeds on all kinds of food, including fruit, insects, and spiders, but it also drinks nectar from eucalyptus flowers. During the breeding season, females carry up to four young in their pouches as they climb high above the ground. A smaller marsupial, the honey possum from Western Australia relies entirely on nectar for its food.

Strong tail can provide extra grip by hanging onto stalks

Ball of compressed pollen in basket of stiff hairs

Feet with opposable thumbs and nonslip pads on all five toes

Eucalytpus flower with no petals, but feathery stamens, which brush pollen onto animals

Big, broad wing creates a lot of lift, allowing bat to maneuver tightly around flower

Protruding stamen brushes pollen onto bat's muzzle and tongue as it feeds

Double diet

When honeybees visit flowers, they collect food in two ways. They drink nectar with their long tongues and at the same time they gather pollen on their body hairs. Every few seconds, a bee moistens its forelegs, then uses them to comb the pollen into baskets on its hind legs. When these are full, it carries the nectar and pollen back to the hive. Here, the nectar is used to make honey—an energy-rich food stored in honeycombs. Pollen is used mainly to feed developing bee grubs.

Perfect fit

For more than 100 million years, flowering plants have evolved in step with their insect visitors. Some flowers are pollinated by a variety of insects, but the shape of others fits only one particular partner. Darwin's hawk moth of Madagascar has a tongue 12 in (30 cm) long. It visits flowers with extra-long nectar-tubes, or spurs, which are pollinated by it alone.

Long-spurred orchid flower

Tongue, normally coiled up during flight, unrolled while feeding

Eating fruit and seeds

Compared to leaves, fruit and seeds are packed with nutrients, which is why many animals use them as food. In warm parts of the world, fruit grows all year round. Elsewhere, it is seasonal, so animals have to switch to different foods when the yearly harvest comes to an end. Seeds are different, because they often keep for a long time. Animals can either eat them right away or put them in private storage.

Inside job

This weevil grub, peering out of an acorn, grows up inside its food. It eats the acorn as it grows and stays inside it until it falls. Once the acorn hits the ground, the grub crawls out and burrows into the soil. Here, it turns into an adult weevil (a kind of beetle), ready to lay its eggs on acorns the following year. This two-stage life cycle is very common in insects. Many different insects grow inside the seeds of cultivated plants, including cereals, peas, and beans.

Meal on the move

Fruit is the most important item on the orangutan menu. In their natural habitat—the rain forests of Southeast Asia—orangutans eat dozens of species of wild fig, as well as durians, lychees, and rambutans. Each tree fruits at a different time of year and the apes move to follow the pattern of ripening. Fewer fruits ripen during the dry season, so orangutans turn to alternative foods, such as leaves and insects. Some use sticks to get at seeds—a skill they pick up by watching and copying each other. Unlike chimps and gorillas, orangutans spend most of their lives in the treetops and only occasionally come down to the ground.

Final feast

Attracted by its smell, this European hornet is feeding on a ripe fig. During spring and summer, hornets hunt other insects, which they feed to their grubs. As summer comes to an end, there are no more grubs left to feed, and they switch to feeding on fruit. However, this feast is often short-lived. Unlike queen hornets, worker hornets do not hibernate—instead, most of them die with the first frosts.

Sensitive antenna detects sugary scents carried on the air

Digesting seeds

Birds do not have teeth, so they cannot chew seeds or other foods. Instead, they often swallow small seeds whole, after removing the husk. The food then enters a storage chamber called the crop, before moving to the gizzard—a muscular chamber that grinds it up. Birds often swallow stones, which become lodged in their gizzard, helping it to break up the food.

Kidney removes waste from blood

Esophagus carries food to crop

Gizzard grinds up food

Intestine absorbs nutrients

Crop stores food

Cloaca expels all waste

Anatomy of a pigeon

Top half of beak hinges with skull

Tongue

Narrow tip of beak digs kernels out of nuts

Foot with four fleshy toes tipped with long claws

Outdoor pantry

Many mammals and birds store seeds. Acorn woodpeckers make their stores out in the open, by jamming acorns into holes that they drill in trees. They work in groups, filling their store with up to 50,000 acorns, which they carefully guard. Many other birds store seeds by burying them in the ground. Amazingly, they can remember the location of thousands of seeds, months after they were hidden away.

Nutcracker

The hyacinth macaw is the largest flying parrot, with the strongest beak of any bird. It can exert a pressure of 2,100 lb per sq in (150 kg per square cm), enough to crack open extra-hard palm nuts. Like other parrots, it uses its feet to hold its food, while it turns nuts into the right position with its stubby tongue.

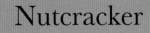

Jaws crush food into a pulp before it is swallowed

Omnivores

Most animals are either plant-eaters or predators and rarely change from their usual food. Instead of keeping to the same menu, omnivores eat anything edible they can find. They include a diverse range of animals, from cockroaches to the mighty brown bear, which is the world's largest omnivore, sometimes weighing more than half a ton. Whatever their size, omnivores are adaptable and adventurous and are ready to try foods they have not eaten before. Some omnivores have become successful at life in towns, where they thrive on leftovers that omnivorous humans throw away.

Fatal leap

Every spring, Alaska's brown bears wade into rivers during the annual salmon run, when adult salmon migrate upstream to spawn (produce eggs). It is a major event in the brown bear's calendar, because fish is a very nutritious food. Dozens of bears gather at fast-flowing rapids, grabbing salmon as they leap into the air. This yearly feast shows in the brown bear's size. Alaska's brown bears, or "grizzlies," are often twice as heavy as those that live in other regions, where there are few fish to catch.

Bear necessities

Brown bears live across the northern hemisphere. Their diet depends on the time of year and varies from place to place. In Alaska and on the coast of eastern Russia, brown bears get more than one-tenth of their yearly food from fish. They also eat other animals, including deer and huge numbers of insect grubs. Despite their hunting skills, plants make up about three-quarters of their food.

Vegetation

Seeds and fruit

Shellfish

Fish

Mammals, birds, and insects

A nose for food

Most omnivorous mammals are active after dark and track down food by its smell. Wild boar search for food mainly at dusk and dawn. They use smell to find acorns and berries among fallen leaves and hunt small animals, such as mice, birds, and beetles. They also sniff out food that is hidden underground. A wild boar's snout works like a shovel, pushing aside the soil so that it can get at roots, fungi, grubs, and worms, as well as dead remains. In times of food shortage, they can dig up farmed crops such as corn.

Not too picky

Together with their close relatives—ravens, jays, and magpies—crows are intelligent birds with an appetite for all kinds of food. Crows cannot chew, so they must smash many meals, such as this turtle, on hard objects, or swallow them whole. Compared to mammals, crows have a poor sense of smell and find their food by sight. They raid the nests of other birds to eat their eggs and young, and they like to steal bright or shiny objects that catch their eye.

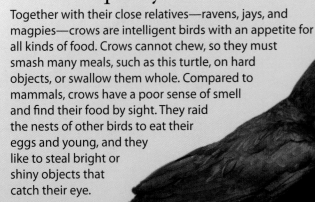

Young redbelly turtle with hard shell

Space invaders

Many omnivorous mammals live in built-up areas, or even inside buildings. Aside from insects, the most successful of these omnivores are mammals. They can live alongside people without being seen, because they are mainly active at night. Humans can find raccoons and foxes a nuisance, because they upturn garbage cans and make a mess, but rats are a more serious problem, since they can spread disease.

Brown rat
The brown rat lives all over the world. Its favorite foods include grain and other seeds, but it eats all kinds of other things, from chicken bones to soap. Brown rats can breed all year round if they have enough food.

Raccoon
In North America, the raccoon sorts through garbage using its small but sensitive front paws. Its natural habitat is woodland, and it thrives in built-up areas wherever there are trees. In addition to eating leftovers, it digs up garden plants and pulls fish out of backyard ponds.

Red fox
Urban foxes are widespread in Europe and North America, even in busy city centers. Moving briskly, they can cover up to 6 miles (10 km) a night in their search for food. Red foxes usually forage after dark, but they often stay up after dawn before returning to their dens.

Animal cannibals

Most predators instinctively avoid targeting their own kind as prey. But some omnivores are not so particular—given an opportunity, they sometimes attack, kill, and eat each other. This Mormon cricket, of the deserts of North America, has done exactly that, and is halfway through its gruesome meal. Mormon crickets usually feed on plants, but they turn on one another if they swarm and start to run out of food. This kind of cannibalism is rare, but many more omnivores—such as slugs—eat the already dead remains of their own kind.

Powerful jaws help to break through body armor

Cricket turned on its back to reveal soft body parts

Filter-feeders

Instead of hunting animals one by one, filter-feeders strain food from the water around them. This way of feeding is very efficient and is used by many animals in freshwater and the oceans. The biggest by far is the blue whale, which feeds mainly on finger-sized crustaceans called krill. Filter-feeders also include birds, fish, and worms, as well as huge numbers of other invertebrates, from mussels and barnacles on rocky shores to jellylike salps in the seas. Most filter-feeders eat live animals and microorganisms, but some behave more like scavengers. They sieve particles of dead matter that drift with the currents or that fall down from the surface waters above.

Record appetite

The blue whale is the world's largest eating machine, growing up to 100 ft (30 m) long. Instead of teeth, it has filters made of baleen that hang from its upper jaw. When a blue whale finds a swarm of krill, it plows through them with its mouth open, while its throat expands like a balloon. It then closes its mouth and presses with its throat and tongue. The water is squeezed out, but the krill are trapped by the baleen and then swallowed. With this filtering system, a blue whale can gulp down 1 ton of food in a single meal.

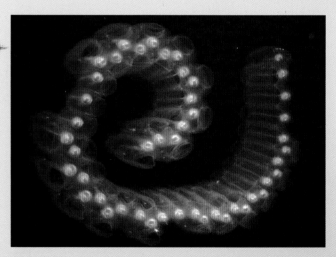

Muscular pleats tighten to force water out of mouth

Fish filters

With their mouths held open, these striped mackerel are using their gills to breathe and to feed. As they swim, they trap small animals with special gill rakers that are like teeth in a tiny comb. Filter-feeding fish include herrings, anchovies, and sardines, but this way of feeding is also used by some giants of the fish world. The largest of them all, the whale shark, grows up to 46 ft (14 m) long. It cruises through tropical seas, scooping up crustaceans, small fish, and squid.

Heads down

Flamingos are the only birds that eat entirely by filter-feeding. They live in salty lakes and lagoons and use their strangely shaped beaks to collect shrimp and microscopic plants. A flamingo's tongue works like a pump, pushing water through the edges of its beak, which is lined with fibrous plates that trap its food. Young flamingos have straight beaks and feed on a milky fluid produced by their parents.

Flamingo feeding by sweeping upside-down beak from side to side

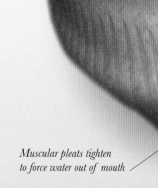

Mysterious life

This strange object is a chain of salps. These filter-feeders are close relatives of sea squirts, but instead of spending their adult lives fixed in one place, they move through the sea. Their bodies are shaped like hollow tubes, with muscles to pump water and a sieve to collect food. A chain of salps can contain hundreds of animals and grow many yards long and thicker than a human leg. Eventually, this breaks up, and individual salps produce eggs that start new chains.

Water surging out through narrow gap between jaws, leaving krill trapped inside mouth

Baleen plates at rear of jaw measure up to 3⅓ ft (1 m) from base to tip

Tongue retracts when whale opens mouth to feed

Sitting sieves

In the sea, many filter-feeders spend their adult lives fastened in one place. This peacock worm collects particles of food with its feathery tentacles, which are covered with microscopic hairs. The worm lives in a tube, which it makes from grit and mud. It is very sensitive to disturbance and if danger threatens, its tentacles fold up like a fan and instantly disappear.

Trap jaw

A blue whale has up to 400 whalebone, or baleen, plates hanging from each side of its upper jaw. Baleen is made of a fibrous protein called keratin. The outside of each plate is hard and stiff, but the side facing inward is frayed, like the bristles of a brush. These bristles overlap, creating a giant sieve along each side of the whale's head. It lets water out and traps food inside.

Free ride

Instead of swimming around to find food, remoras can fasten themselves to larger fish, using a suckerlike pad on the tops of their heads. Sometimes they hitchhike alone, but here more than 20 have latched on to a fully grown whale shark and are using its immense muscle power to get a lift through the sea. Remoras remove parasites from the whale's skin to feed on and can unstick themselves whenever they want. They dart out to catch leftover food scraps or to feed on the waste that their host squirts into the water as it swims.

Scavengers and recyclers

When predators feed on their prey, they often leave parts of their kill. When they have moved on, scavengers arrive to eat the food that has not been used. Scavengers eat all kinds of remains, including animals that have died through accidents or disease, and they play a key part in nature by helping to return nutrients to the soil. Large scavengers, such as hyenas and vultures, tear the remains apart. As time goes by, many smaller animals chew and burrow their way through fur, skin, and muscle, until only scattered bones are left.

Soil microlife

Soil contains enormous numbers of animals that feed on dead remains, and also on each other. Some of them—such as earthworms and burrowing centipedes—are easy to see, but many others are almost invisible to the naked eye. This springtail feeds on tiny particles of organic matter, or detritus. Most springtails are less than ¼ in (5 mm) long, but they are among the world's most abundant animals.

Powerful lappet-faced vulture has a 10-ft (3-m) wingspan

Crowded carcass

As soon as the air warms up after sunrise, vultures take to the skies watching for signs of food. Their eyesight is sharp, and they descend within minutes if they spot a meal. Here, a group of vultures has gathered around a lion's kill. The lappet-faced vulture, on top of the carcass, is bald, which helps to keep it clean as it feeds. It tears open the hide, allowing smaller vultures to reach inside.

Diet of dung

Watched by its partner, a male African dung beetle creates a ball by rolling the dung of large mammals. The ball is up to 2 in (5 cm) across, and the beetles will bury it to create a food store for their young. Dung beetles have a keen sense of smell and are some of nature's most efficient recyclers. Thanks to their work, dung produced by rhinos and elephants disappears within a few days.

Hard bone containing soft bone marrow

Bone breaker

After teeth, bones are the hardest parts of dead remains. They may look unappetizing, but they contain bone marrow—a soft and nutritious food. Hyenas crush bones with their super-strong jaws, and then swallow the pieces with the rest of their food, which includes skin and hooves. Inside the hyena's body, powerful stomach acids dissolve the bone, so that it travels through the digestive system without doing any harm. A hyena's stomach acids also kill bacteria, letting it feed on rotting meat without becoming sick.

White-backed vulture with short feathers on head and neck

Complete carcass	Hyena
	Top scavengers
Dismembered carcass	Vulture
	2nd-level scavengers
Coarse fragments	Burying beetle
	3rd-level scavengers
Fine Fragments	Springtail
	Detritivores
Detritus	Earthworm
	Detritivores

Breaking down remains

Scavengers work like an assembly line in reverse, breaking down dead remains. Top scavengers, such as hyenas, feed on large pieces of food. At the other end of the scale, detritivores, such as springtails and earthworms, feed on the tiny particles that become mixed up in the soil. This is not the end of the story, because detritivores produce waste as they feed. This waste is processed by microscopic fungi and bacteria, which keep soil fertile, helping plants to grow.

Submerged scavengers

In water, dead remains eventually sink, so most of the scavengers live on the seabed or in the sediment on muddy shores. This rock is covered by brittle stars, which scavenge food by reaching upward with several arms, while the remaining arms hold them in place. Each arm is covered with sticky mucus, which traps particles of food drifting down. In deeper parts of the ocean, brittle stars often feed on dead fish. They wriggle their way toward it across the seabed, attracted by its scent.

Hunters and hunted

Solitary hunters

The animal world is a place of constant danger, because predators are never far away. Some of them work in groups, but most hunt on their own, using specialized weapons to catch and kill their prey. They include animals that run their prey down or stealthily track their victims, and ones that do the exact opposite—keep still and wait for food to come within their reach. However they hunt, all predators have lightning-fast reactions— the key to making a successful kill.

Death in the trees

In the forests of Costa Rica, a venomous eyelash viper stabs a mouse with its fangs. This brightly colored snake lives in trees and bushes, from where it ambushes rodents, lizards, tree frogs, and birds. The viper's reactions are so quick that it can grab hummingbirds as they hover in front of flowers. Its powerful venom paralyzes its prey within seconds, making it easy for the snake to swallow whole.

Mouse hangs paralyzed by viper's venomous bite

Fatal fling

A young seal out at sea is easy prey for a great white shark. Bursting up to the surface from below, the shark hits its victim with such force that the seal is thrown out of the water before being snatched in the shark's large jaws. The shark is effectively camouflaged by its two-tone coloring, which makes it difficult to spot in the water from both above and below.

Patient killer

The praying mantis is a sit-and-wait killer that blends in well among the twigs and leaves. It rests with its front legs folded together, turning its head in all directions to watch for passing insects. If an insect lands within range, the mantis slowly leans forward, then strikes with its front legs. Their tips snap together, trapping its prey between rows of spines like jagged knives. The mantis starts to feed immediately, while its live victim struggles to escape.

Front legs have inward-pointing spines that impale prey

Black mamba

Dragonfly

Blue marlin

Cheetah

Peregrine falcon

| Animal speeds | 12 mph (20 kph) | | 36 mph (58 kph) | 51 mph (82 kph) | 70 mph (112 kph) | 118 mph (190 kph) |

High-speed attacks

Predators that hunt out in the open need to be fast to catch their prey. The fastest of all is the peregrine falcon, which preys on other birds by dive-bombing, or stooping, them in midair. The blue marlin is one of the fastest lone hunters in the water, while the cheetah is the fastest predator on land.

Wing feather has soft fringes that muffle sound

Silent swoop

Despite its impressive wingspan, the great gray owl is an almost silent hunter. It lives in the northern forests of Europe, North America, and Asia and feeds on small rodents, swooping down from the trees on its unsuspecting victims. In the winter, the great gray owl catches prey in the snow. The bird has extremely sensitive hearing, and it can even home in on rodents hiding below the surface, using its weight to punch its way through the frozen crust.

Forest stalker

Like most members of the cat family, the jaguar hunts with stealth. Hidden among the trees, the jaguar stalks its prey by watching and listening for signs of movement on the forest floor. The jaguar weighs up to 330 lb (150 kg) and is strong enough to catch deer and alligators, but it also eats smaller animals, including fish, turtles, and birds. Big cats usually kill their prey by grasping their throats and suffocating them, but the jaguar uses its sharp canine teeth to crush its victims' skulls.

91

Making a splash

Many birds dive-bomb fish at sea, but the common
kingfisher catches its prey in freshwater. It needs clear
water to hunt and spots fish by watching carefully
from a perch. If it sees a fish, it may dive right away,
but often it hovers, gauging the fish's exact position.
Once ready, the kingfisher plunges into the water with
its beak slightly open. A split-second later, it carries the
fish back to its perch. The bird stuns the fish with a few
sharp blows against the perch and swallows it headfirst.

Hunting together

When hunting alone, predators can catch only those animals that they are strong enough to overpower. However, by joining forces with other members of the same species, some animals are able to kill prey many times their own size. Other hunters work together to round up animals on land, or in water, making prey easier to catch. Cooperative hunting has evolved in a wide range of predators, from army ants to humpback whales. Animals that hunt together are often close relatives, and many remain in the same group for the whole of their lives.

Army on the move

Attacked from all sides by army ants, this tiger moth has no chance of escape. Army ants live in giant family groups up to 20 million strong. They swarm across the forest floor, hunting down any small animal that crosses their path.

Bubble netting

Humpback whales feed on fish and krill and have a unique way of rounding up their prey. Several whales will come together and swim in a wide circle around a shoal of fish. One, or more, of the whales blows a wall of bubbles in the water, which confuses the fish and drives them into the center of the trap. Gradually, the whales tighten the net of bubbles, before lunging upward through the shoal and swallowing huge mouthfuls of food.

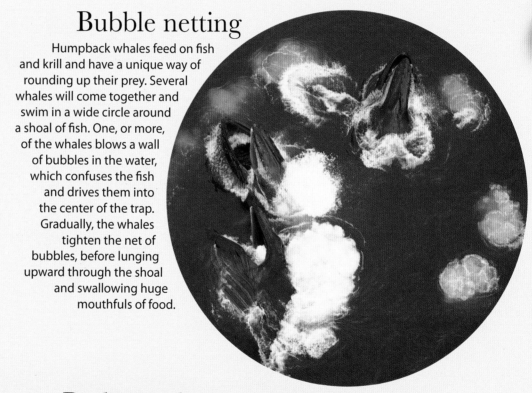

Pelican trap

Pelicans are different from most other water birds in that they fish together in organized flocks. These Australian pelicans have located a shoal of fish and driven them into shallow water by beating the surface with their wings. With the shoal trapped in the shallows, the pelicans jostle for their share of the feast, scooping up fish in their large, pouched beaks.

Pack attack

By working together as a pack, African wild dogs can hunt down a wildebeest that is five times bigger than they are. They chase their prey until it is exhausted and then bring it down with a coordinated attack, which often starts when one dog grabs the wildebeest's hind leg or tail. These dogs are very effective hunters—more than three-quarters of their pack attacks result in a successful kill.

*Fish pack together
for protection*

Underwater roundup

Herded together by a pod of common dolphins, this shoal of fish instinctively tightens up into a whirling mass called a bait ball. The dolphins speed around the boundaries of the ball and then take turns plunging through its center, grabbing the slippery fish with their pointed teeth. Dolphins communicate with a complex language of whistles and clicks, which helps to coordinate their attack.

Chimpanzee ambush

Chimpanzees eat almost every kind of food, from leaves and fruit to bird's eggs and young animals. Most of the animals they catch are small, but in some parts of Africa, chimpanzees work together to chase down colobus monkeys high up in trees. Colobus monkeys are the more agile climbers, but a hunting party of chimpanzees can outwit them by planning an ambush. Some of the chimpanzees hide in the treetops, while a driver surprises their prey, setting the trap in motion. The monkey victim tries to escape through the trees, but it is steered along a path by chimps that block its escape on either side. Together, the chimps drive the prey toward a hidden ambusher, which makes the final kill.

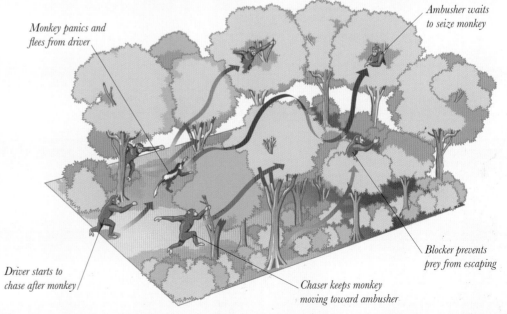

*Monkey panics and
flees from driver*

*Ambusher waits
to seize monkey*

*Driver starts to
chase after monkey*

*Chaser keeps monkey
moving toward ambusher*

*Blocker prevents
prey from escaping*

Gaping jaws swallow prey nearly half fish's own size

Traps and tricks

Instead of chasing their food, the animal world's most specialized hunters use traps to catch their prey. Trappers work in all types of habitat, from the soil to the deep sea. Spiders and ant lions build their lairs themselves, but some predators have body parts that act as lures—attracting unsuspecting victims toward their jaws. A few hunters even use bait to bring their prey within reach.

Fatal lights

Bioluminescent barbel produces steady light, which attracts prey

In the permanent darkness of the ocean depths, many predators hunt by trailing luminous lures. This scaly dragonfish has a glowing whisker, called a bioluminescent barbel, which hangs from its jaws and attracts smaller fish toward its mouth. Some deep-sea fish use bioluminescent bacteria to make their light, but the dragonfish creates its own, using a light-emitting chemical called luciferin. Its prey are often luminous as well, so the dragonfish has a black stomach lining to stop other predators from homing in on fish that it has swallowed.

Deadly doors

Unlike web-making spiders, a trapdoor spider hunts by ambushing its prey on the ground. It builds a tunnel equipped with a hinged lid made from silk and particles of soil. The spider then waits hidden at the top of its burrow, with the door slightly ajar. If an insect walks past, the spider feels the vibrations and immediately reacts. In a split second, it throws open the door, grabs its prey, and then pulls it underground. After slamming the door shut, the spider starts to feed.

Fishing with bait

Many birds eat fish, but the green heron is one of the few that catches them using bait. It scatters twigs, feathers, insects, and other small objects on the water's surface and then stabs any fish that arrive to take a closer look. The bird's behavior is even more remarkable because it seems to be learned—some green herons never acquire this special hunting technique.

Water jet knocks insect down to waiting archerfish

Living lure

When young, a Mexican moccasin snake has a brightly colored tip to its wormlike tail. The snake coils up and dangles its lure above its body, wiggling the bait to entice prey closer. Birds fall prey to this venomous snake because they focus entirely on the yellow, moving tail. They fail to notice the rest of the snake, lying camouflaged against the forest floor.

Slippery slopes

In warm regions around the world, sandy ground is often peppered with small, steep-sided holes. These are traps dug out by ant lions—insect grubs that grow up to have long, lacy wings. Ant lions bury themselves at the bottom of the pit and wait for passing prey. If an insect walks near the edge of the hole, the ant lion flicks sand grains at it. The prey loses its footing and tumbles down into the ant lion's open jaws.

Hole up to 1 in (2.5 cm) across

Killer shot

The banded archerfish cruises in the shallows of mangrove swamps, looking to shoot down prey above the water. If it spots an insect on an overhanging leaf, it presses its tongue against a groove in its mouth and quickly snaps shut its gill covers. This forces a jet of water out through its mouth, which knocks the insect off its perch. From under water, the fish have a distorted view of their prey, caused by the light bending as it passes from air to water. However, archerfish are able to compensate for this when they take aim and can hit a target more than 6½ ft (2 m) away.

Gill cover closes rapidly, allowing fish to squirt jets of water

Steep, sandy sides stop insects from climbing out

Ant lion pierces prey and sucks out its juices

Feeding on blood

Blood is the ideal meal for many animals—it is rich in all kinds of nutrients, and it is easy to digest. Some of the world's most numerous insects feed on blood, particularly at breeding times. Most bloodsucking animals have mouthparts that pierce or slice through skin, and many produce substances that prevent blood from clotting as they feed. Some blood-feeders, such as mosquitoes and vampire bats, move on once they have eaten their fill, but others, known as parasites, often stay aboard their hosts. These hitchhikers, including fleas, ticks, and lice, have tough bodies and can be very difficult to dislodge.

Jumping aboard

Fleas are wingless insects that live on the bodies of mammals and birds, where they suck the blood of their hosts. These tiny parasites measure only 0.04–⅓ in (1–8 mm) in length, yet they can leap more than 12 in (30 cm) from host to host. Once aboard, fleas scuttle through fur or feathers and cling on safely using the long bristles that cover their bodies.

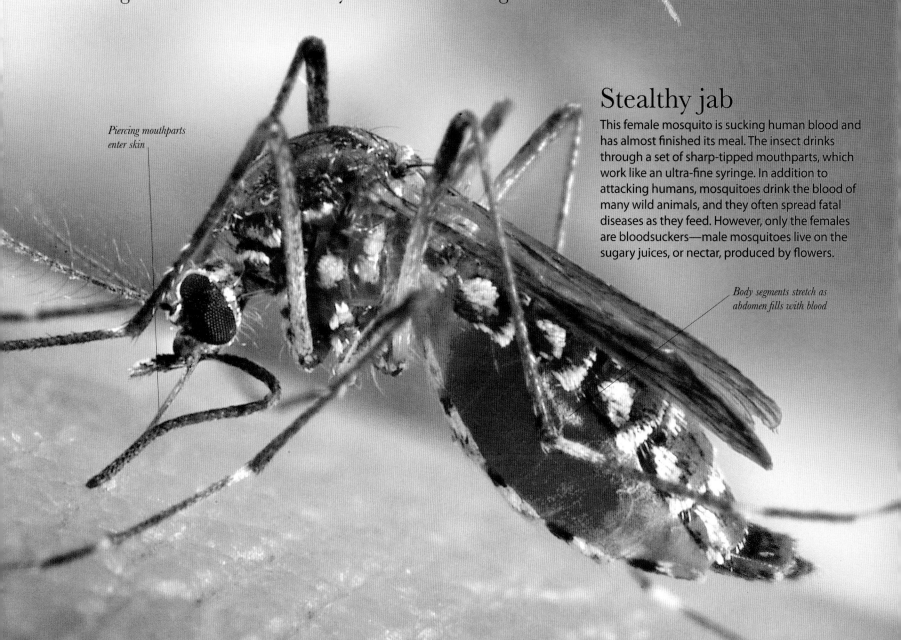

Bulging hind-leg muscles power the flea's jumps

Microscopic view of a cat flea

Stealthy jab

This female mosquito is sucking human blood and has almost finished its meal. The insect drinks through a set of sharp-tipped mouthparts, which work like an ultra-fine syringe. In addition to attacking humans, mosquitoes drink the blood of many wild animals, and they often spread fatal diseases as they feed. However, only the females are bloodsuckers—male mosquitoes live on the sugary juices, or nectar, produced by flowers.

Piercing mouthparts enter skin

Body segments stretch as abdomen fills with blood

Lingering leech

This pike has an uninvited passenger—a fish leech, which uses its suckers to cling on to its host while feeding on its blood. Fish leeches find a host by resting in gravel or mud and stretching upward like plant stems. If a fish passes by, the leech quickly swims toward it and grabs hold with its biting jaws.

Sucker surrounds mouth at narrow end of body

Biting attack

Vampire bats exist in real life, and not just in horror movies. They live in Mexico, Central America, and South America, where they feast on the blood of mammals and birds. When a vampire bat tracks down its prey, it first uses its razor-sharp incisor teeth to bite into the animal's skin. Then the bat drinks its fill by lapping up the blood that flows from the wound.

Massive meal

Female sheep ticks have abdomens that stretch like balloons as they feed on blood. Adult females feed just once, taking a week or more to complete their meal. The tick's body weight increases by up to 50 times, and it can be as large as a grape. Once full, the tick drops off to lay its eggs on the ground.

Sheep tick
before feeding

Sheep tick
after feeding

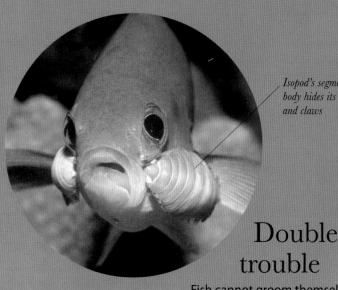

Isopod's segmented body hides its legs and claws

Double trouble

Fish cannot groom themselves, which makes them easy targets for bloodsucking parasites. This host fish is being attacked by two isopods, which are sea crustaceans related to woodlice. Using their claws, the isopods have firmly latched on to the fish's head and are feeding on blood from the soft flesh near its gills.

Finch pecks at base of tail feathers, making blood flow

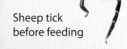

Blood-thirsty bird

The sharp-beaked ground finch of the Galápagos Islands has a rare feeding habit among birds—it drinks the blood of living animals. This finch attacks boobies and other large sea birds, perching on their backs while it feeds. This behavior has earned the bird the nickname "vampire finch," even though it eats mainly insects and seeds.

Camouflage and mimicry

For both predators and prey, camouflage can be a vital weapon in the fight to stay alive. Camouflage helps hunters to get close to their food, but it also protects prey from their predators by making them harder to find. Many animals use camouflage to hide and blend in with their surroundings, but some—called mimics—trick their enemies by imitating dangerous animals or inedible objects. Insects lead the animal world in camouflage defense. Many disguise themselves as twigs, leaves, or flowers, but some imitate other creatures that are armed with poisons or painful stings.

Hornet's yellow and brown markings warn that it is dangerous if attacked

Arctic fox in winter

Clearwing moth mimics the hornet's color scheme

Seeing double

It takes an expert eye to tell a clearwing moth from a hornet. Both have yellow and brown markings and long transparent wings, and both make a buzzing sound when they fly. However, despite its menacing look, the clearwing moth is harmless—only the real hornet is armed with a sting. This kind of mimicry is a very effective defense, and it has evolved in many different insects. It is also common in small spiders, which often imitate stinging ants.

Arctic fox in summer

Changing coats

In the Arctic, dark colors stand out against the snowy landscape, particularly during the winter months. Like many polar mammals, most Arctic foxes replace their brown summer coat with a thicker, white winter coat in the fall, so that they stay camouflaged all year round. The fox's color change is triggered by seasonal differences in day length. These alter hormone levels in the fox's blood, which make it grow a new, furry disguise.

Color merging

Chameleons can change their skin color rapidly to hide from prey and to signal to each other when they meet. They do this by expanding and contracting specialized color cells in the skin called chromatophores. The tiny chromatophores contain chemical pigments, and layers of several cells work together to reflect light and create flushes of different colors. The chameleon's nervous system controls these skin changes to mimic its environment or to show its mood.

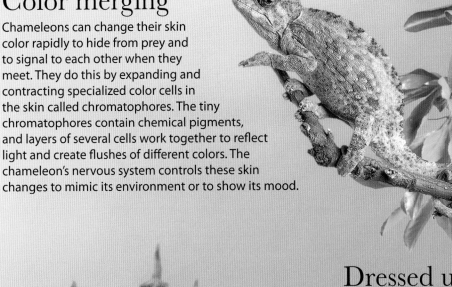

Insect disguises

More than nine-tenths of the world's insects spend their lives on plants, creating a huge food supply for insect-eating predators. The insects have evolved an incredible variety of disguises that help to make them almost invisible to hunters, even when seen up close. Large numbers of these plant-dwellers move and feed mostly after dark to keep from giving themselves away.

Leaf mimic
With its flattened body and mottled green markings, a leaf insect, or phylliid, looks almost identical to a real leaf. When it moves, it sways gently from side to side, just like a leaf rustling in the breeze.

Fake flower
In warm regions of the world, flower mantises lurk among colorful blooms, waiting for other insects to come their way. Their bodies are usually white or brightly marked, and they often have petal-like flaps on their legs.

Bark blender
Many moths seem to disappear the moment they land on bark. Their wings and bodies are colored like tree bark, and they may have contrasting stripes that break up their outline, making them even harder to see.

False thorns
Thorn bugs have a curved spike on their thoraxes, which looks exactly like a plant thorn. If a predator manages to see through this disguise, the spike makes the bugs very difficult to eat.

Living twig
The caterpillars of geometer moths look like tiny twigs covered with gray-brown bark. To complete the disguise, they rest with their bodies sloping outward, just like a real twig forking from a branch.

Dressed up

Decorator crabs conceal themselves by attaching living animals to their bodies. This tropical species is called a soft coral crab because it collects pieces of coral to camouflage its shell. Tiny hooks on the crab's exoskeleton hold the corals firmly in place as they grow to form a living disguise. Unlike most camouflaged animals, decorator crabs lose their disguise when they molt. To save time and energy, the crabs usually remove the camouflage from their old exoskeleton and carefully arrange it on their new one.

Crab's coloring blends in with its soft-coral covering

Vanishing trick

Many animals mimic dead leaves and rely on their camouflage as protection against predators, but one particular lizard is a master of this type of disguise. The leaf-tailed gecko lives in the forests of Madagascar and is almost impossible to spot among the dead leaves in the trees and on the forest floor. Its dark body is marked with ribs and veins, while its leaf-shaped tail has notched edges, as if it has been nibbled by caterpillars. The gecko is active at night, feeding on a diet of insects. During the day, it keeps motionless so that it magically disappears from sight.

Stings and venom

When a rattlesnake goes hunting, it has no need to overpower its prey. Instead, it stabs its victim with its fangs and then waits while its deadly venom sets to work. Poisoning is an efficient and safe method of killing because it prevents prey from fighting back. Snakes are among the largest animals with a poisonous bite, but animals with a toxic sting outnumber them by far. The most deadly animal poisons are not produced for hunting—instead, they provide poison dart frogs with the ultimate means of self-defense.

Toad inflates itself with air and tilts body to look bigger

Poison gland

Standoff

When confronted by a snake, a cane toad puffs up its body and stands its ground, instead of trying to escape. It has bulging glands just behind its eyes that ooze poisons onto its skin. The poisons protect the toad from most predators, although some snakes are immune to its effects. Originally from the American tropics, the cane toad's growing population has become a major problem in Australia, where it has no natural enemies.

Wasp's sting withdraws into abdomen when not in use

Killer cones

Most sea snails are slow-moving animals and are also ponderous feeders. Cone snails overcome these physical disadvantages by paralyzing their prey with toxic venom. They impale passing fish and other animals with their harpoonlike mouthparts and inject them with poison. This cone snail has caught a blenny and is using its foot to haul in its meal.

Stinging cells

Jellyfish and their relatives have trailing tentacles armed with batteries of stinging cells, called cnidocytes. There is a poison-tipped thread coiled up inside each cell and a trigger hair on the outside. When prey touches the trigger, the stinging thread explodes outward and impales the victim. After firing, the cnidocyte is replaced by a new cell.

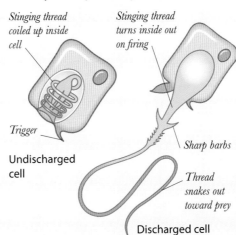

Stinging thread coiled up inside cell

Stinging thread turns inside out on firing

Trigger

Undischarged cell

Sharp barbs

Thread snakes out toward prey

Discharged cell

Deadly trail

The Portuguese man-of-war has a gas-filled float, trailing tentacles up to 20 ft (6 m) long. Each tentacle is covered with thousands of cnidocytes, which fire if they make contact with prey. The tentacles then contract to haul in the food.

Lethal skin

In the forests of Central and South America, poison dart frogs use brilliant colors to warn predators that they are highly dangerous. All of them have poisonous skins, and some kinds produce batrachotoxin, which is the most powerful poison in the animal world. In the Amazon, human forest-dwellers traditionally use the poison when hunting. Just 0.000035 oz (1 mg) of the poison, smeared on the tip of a blowpipe dart, is more than enough to kill a monkey or sloth.

Foldaway fangs

A snake's fangs are specialized teeth that inject venom into its prey. Many snakes have fixed fangs, but those of rattlesnakes and their relatives are hinged and swing forward as they bite. Snake venom works in different ways. Some kinds act on the prey's nervous system, stopping the heart and lungs from working and paralyzing muscles. Rattlesnake venom cuts off its victim's circulation by clotting the blood. Snake venom is not always injected—spitting cobras defend themselves by firing it through the air and into their attacker's eyes.

Hollow fang injects venom

Paralyzing poison

After stinging a spider, a female spider-hunting wasp drags its prey away to its burrow. The spider is not dead, but is paralyzed by the wasp's venom, which prevents it from fighting back. Once in the burrow, the wasp will lay an egg on the spider. In the days that follow, the egg will hatch, and the wasp grub will feed on its living food supply.

Animal armor

When sudden danger strikes, many animals rely on their speed to escape from trouble and make a dash for safety. Others have special body protection that helps them survive a surprise attack or defend themselves from hungry predators. Armadillos are protected by bony plates, but many other animals use armored shells, sharp spines, or thick hides to hold their enemies at bay. Horns and antlers can also fend off predators, but their main use is in ritual mating battles between rival males.

Armored ball

All species of armadillo have defensive armor made of interlocking bony plates, which protects their backs, heads, and parts of their legs and tail. If attacked, many armadillos try to run or dig their way to safety, but the three-banded armadillo stands its ground. This mammal can roll its flexible shell into a tight, impenetrable ball.

Prickly defenses

Spines and spikes make animals very difficult for predators to eat. Many animals have spines that stay upright all the time, but some are able to raise their spines as temporary protection when danger threatens.

Thorns
The thorny devil of Australia is a desert lizard covered with sharply pointed scales. In addition to being armored, it is well camouflaged against the desert sand.

Spikes
The porcupinefish raises its spikes by swallowing water, which makes its body swell up like a ball. When its body deflates, the fish's spines lie flat once more.

Spines
Sea urchins have chalky spines attached to raised knobs on their cases. The spines snap easily, embedding themselves in a predator's skin.

Prickles
A hedgehog's prickles are extra-thick hairs with sharp tips. If it is in danger, a hedgehog raises its spines and curls up into a tight, prickly ball.

Armor plating

The Indian rhinoceros is built like a living tank, with thick folds of armored skin. On its hind quarters and legs, the skin is reinforced with swellings that look like rivets, making it tougher still. Thanks to this armored suit, adult rhinos have no natural predators, but many fall victim to poachers, who hunt them for their horns.

Portable protection

Giant tortoises from the Galápagos Islands can weigh nearly one-third of a ton and have the biggest and heaviest shells of all land animals. Like all tortoises, they have soft shells when they first hatch, because the shell's bony plates are not joined together. As a tortoise grows, the plates start to fuse, giving the domed shell its tremendous strength. Most tortoises pull their heads and legs straight back into their shells to avoid danger. Long-necked tortoises bend their heads sideways to fit under their shells.

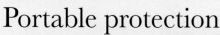

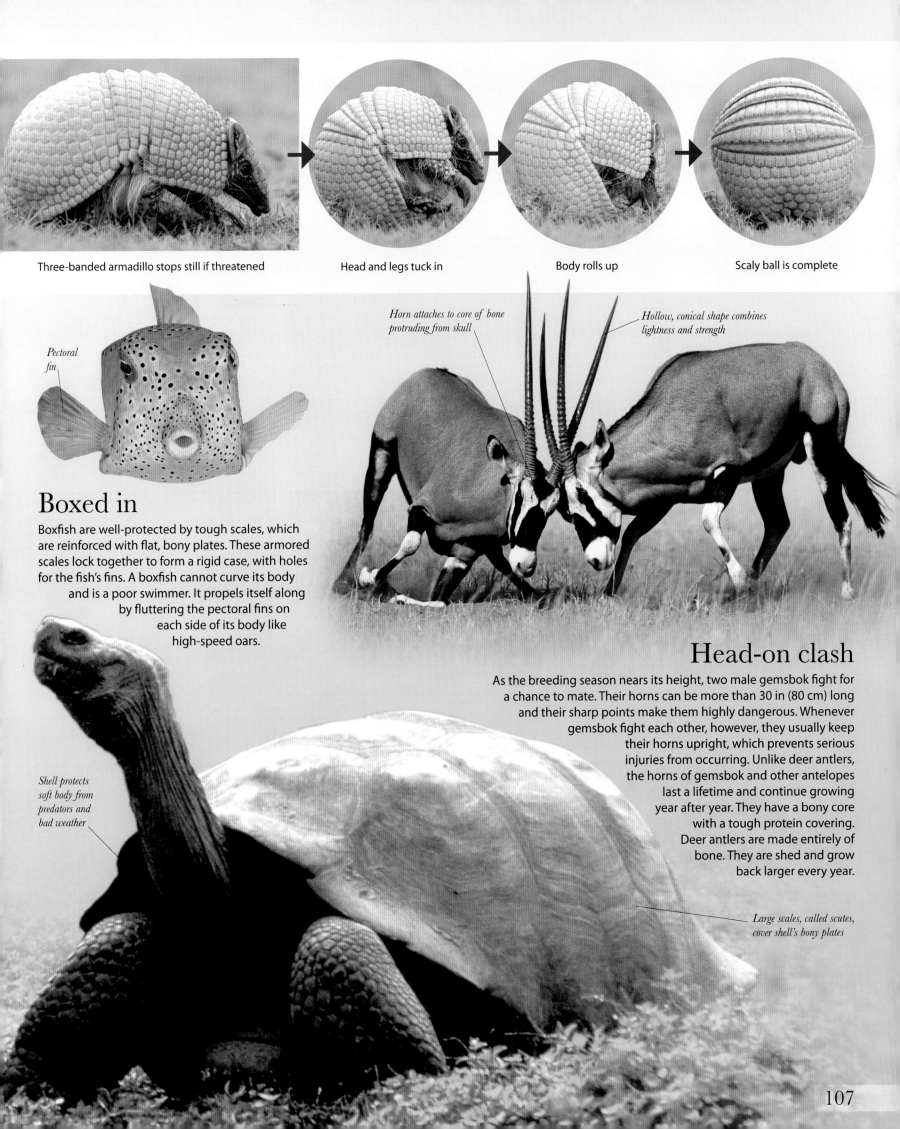

Three-banded armadillo stops still if threatened

Head and legs tuck in

Body rolls up

Scaly ball is complete

Pectoral fin

Boxed in

Boxfish are well-protected by tough scales, which are reinforced with flat, bony plates. These armored scales lock together to form a rigid case, with holes for the fish's fins. A boxfish cannot curve its body and is a poor swimmer. It propels itself along by fluttering the pectoral fins on each side of its body like high-speed oars.

Horn attaches to core of bone protruding from skull

Hollow, conical shape combines lightness and strength

Head-on clash

As the breeding season nears its height, two male gemsbok fight for a chance to mate. Their horns can be more than 30 in (80 cm) long and their sharp points make them highly dangerous. Whenever gemsbok fight each other, however, they usually keep their horns upright, which prevents serious injuries from occurring. Unlike deer antlers, the horns of gemsbok and other antelopes last a lifetime and continue growing year after year. They have a bony core with a tough protein covering. Deer antlers are made entirely of bone. They are shed and grow back larger every year.

Shell protects soft body from predators and bad weather

Large scales, called scutes, cover shell's bony plates

107

Emergency escapes

If an animal's life is in danger, adopting an unusual escape technique can make the difference between life and death. Sailfin lizards hurl themselves off branches and run away across rivers and streams. Beetles sometimes pull in their legs and roll downhill. Many other animals go to even greater extremes and abandon parts of their bodies, while a few simply pretend to be dead. These escape tactics are used against predators only as a last resort, but they often work because they have surprise on their side.

Indonesian sailfin lizard

Ink cloud squirts out of funnel beneath octopus's head

Cloud cover

When danger threatens, an octopus can release a jet of water stained black by "ink." The dark cloud distracts or envelops its attacker, while the octopus makes a speedy getaway. Octopus ink is produced in a sac that forms part of the animal's digestive system. The ink contains highly concentrated melanin—the same chemical pigment that many animals have in their skin or fur.

Playing dead

To escape from attack, the Virginia opossum flops over on its side with its eyes and mouth open, looking as if it has suddenly died. This trick looks suicidal, but it works because most predators eat live prey and choose to leave dead animals alone. Once the hunter has lost interest and moved on, the opossum cautiously comes back to life.

On guard

Propped up by their tails, adult meerkats take turns standing and watching out for predators, while the rest of their pack relaxes or plays. Eagles and hawks pose the biggest danger. If a sentry spots a predator, it barks a specific alarm call, and the meerkats quickly disappear into their burrows.

Walking on water

Kicking out with its large, hind feet, a sailfin lizard splashes its way to safety by sprinting across the surface of a stream. This escape technique works best in early life. Young lizards can race over water for short distances of about 16 ft (5 m) because their bodies are small and light. Slower-moving adults soon start to sink and have to switch to swimming instead.

Foot kicks backward

Follow me

Plovers nest on the ground, where there is danger all around. If a predator approaches its nest, the parent bird stages a distraction display to protect its chicks. The plover pretends to have a broken wing and flutters away from the nest, luring the predator off course. Once the predator has moved to a safe distance, the plover flies back to its young.

Losing limbs

In emergencies, many animals can shed arms, legs, or tails, which helps them flee to safety. For some animals, the loss is permanent, but often the missing body part gradually grows back.

Tail
The tail of the alligator lizard breaks off easily, leaving a stump. A new tail regrows, but contains cartilage instead of bone.

Tail fracture line

New claw

Claw
A lobster's lost claw will slowly regrow, getting bigger each time the crustacean sheds, or molts, its shell.

Original arm

Regenerating arm

Arm
Starfish that lose arms to a predator are able to grow, or regenerate, new ones in their place. Here, an arm that has broken off is turning into a whole new starfish.

Senses

Eyesight

Animals use senses to avoid danger, to find food, and also to find breeding partners. They may rely on touch, taste, and smell, depending on what they are investigating. For many predators, eyesight, or vision, is the most important sense. Eyes can be smaller than a period or more than 20 in (50 cm) across. Some animals see the world in shades of gray, but many can detect colors, including some that are invisible to us. All this information is passed along nerves, which connect the eyes to the brain. Here, the signals are processed, so that an animal can make sense of what it sees.

All-around view

Dragonflies hunt by sight, chasing other insects through the air. With their flexible necks and large bulging eyes, they can see in almost any direction when they fly. Like all arthropods, they have compound eyes, which are built in a totally different way from the eyes of mammals and other vertebrates. Dragonflies also have three much smaller, simple eyes, or ocelli, which sense the overall level of light.

Compound eyes

The eyes of arthropods are made up of compartments called ommatidia. Each ommatidium senses part of the view and forms a separate image. The animal's brain puts these images together, creating a picture like a mosaic. Dragonflies have up to 30,000 ommatidia, so their pictures are detailed. Compound eyes are good at sensing movement, because the ommatidia trigger in quick succession as something moves past.

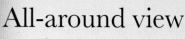

Lens focuses light into an ommatidium

Ommatidium

Nerve carries signals to brain

Look before you leap

This jumping spider pounces on small insects, spotting them with four pairs of eyes. It uses two pairs of sideways-pointing eyes to detect any movement that could spell food. If it sees something move, it turns toward it and focuses with its extra-large median eyes, which give it a very detailed image. Finally, the spider uses two smaller lateral eyes to judge the distance, before suddenly leaping on its prey.

Median eye can swivel to keep the prey directly in the line of sight

Sideways-pointing eyes usually spot prey first

Lateral eye is forward facing and set far apart from the other one, giving good distance judgment

Camera vision

Clinging to a branch, a tarsier sees its rain-forest home through giant eyes. Like those of all other vertebrates, its eyes work like cameras, focusing light on a screen called the retina, which is packed with light-sensitive cells. During the day, its pupils close up to stop it from being dazzled by bright lights. At night, when it hunts, they open wide, letting in as much light as possible.

Pupil narrows in daylight

Night sight

At night, lions' eyes seem to glow when they are caught by a beam of light. This effect is common in nocturnal mammals and also in crocodiles and sharks. It is caused by a reflective layer inside the eye called the tapetum lucidum, which bounces light back through the retina, helping animals to see in the dark. Eyes also adjust to the dark by chemical changes that make them better at sensing dim light.

Beady gaze

Predators often have forward-facing eyes, which are good at judging depth, while plant-eaters tend to have eyes on the sides of their heads, which lets them see danger from all around. Chameleons get the best of both worlds. Their eyes can swivel independently to look all around, but they face forward when the chameleon focuses on its prey.

Amazing eyes

Invertebrate vision
Cuttlefish have a single lens and a retina, like the eyes of mammals and other vertebrates, but have W-shaped pupils.

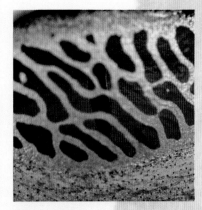

Wipe clean
Red-eyed tree frogs have a mottled third eyelid, or nictitating membrane, which cleans the eye like a windshield wiper.

Lashes of color
Ground hornbills' eyelashes screen their eyes from the Sun's glare and make the eyelids shut instantly when touched.

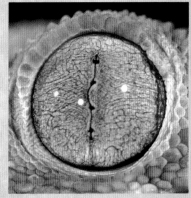

Seeing through a slit
Tokay geckos have slit-shaped pupils in a speckled iris, which camouflages the eye. After dark, their pupils open wide.

Deadly gaze

From its lair in a rocky reef, a mantis shrimp watches for food using the most complex eyes in the animal world. Mounted on stalks, they follow the slightest movement, swiveling independently or fixing potential prey with their unblinking stare. Each eye has 12 different kinds of color-detecting cell—compared to just three in humans—and a highly sensitive central band that analyzes shape and depth. Using this information, the mantis shrimp takes aim and then suddenly grabs its victim with its lethally barbed front legs.

Hearing

The living world is rarely silent. Waves of pressure travel through air, water, and the ground, carrying energy that animals feel as vibrations or hear as sound. Some insects have ears on their antennae, or even on their legs, but in mammals and other vertebrates, the real work of hearing happens once sound is channeled into the head. Here, sensory cells respond to its intensity and pitch (how high or low the sound is), triggering a stream of nerve signals that the brain interprets as sound. For many animals, hearing is essential for communication. Crucially, hearing can reveal the approach of predators, or the exact position of prey.

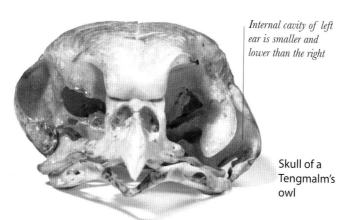

Internal cavity of left ear is smaller and lower than the right

Skull of a Tengmalm's owl

Lopsided ears

Most birds' ears are hidden by the feathers that cover their heads. Despite this, many have extremely good hearing. Far from muffling the sound, the feathers around owls' ears form tunnels that collect and channel the sound like mammals' external ears do. A Tengmalm's owl can track prey using its ears alone. Its two ear cavities are in slightly different positions, which enables it to get an exact "fix" on its target.

Hearing range

A sound's pitch is measured in waves per second, or Hertz (Hz). Humans can sense sounds with a pitch of between 20 and 20,000 Hz, depending on age. Elephants can sense deeper sounds than we can, but many more animals can hear ultrasound, which is sound too high for us to hear. Ultrasonic hearing is important to animals that use echolocation to hunt.

All a-quiver

The antennae of insects are multipurpose sense organs. Fruit flies have antennae that sense air currents and gravity, but they also act as ears. Each antenna has a single branching hair. Sound waves make the hair vibrate, activating a hearing organ. When a male fruit fly courts a female, it vibrates one of its wings. The female senses this with her antennae and lets him mate.

Club-shaped antenna

Branching hair picks up airborne sound waves

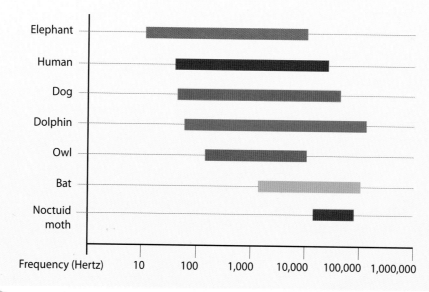

Animal	Frequency (Hertz)
Elephant	
Human	
Dog	
Dolphin	
Owl	
Bat	
Noctuid moth	

Frequency (Hertz)   10   100   1,000   10,000   100,000   1,000,000

Insect ears

Insects have ears in a range of different body parts. Despite this, their ears often work in a similar way. Many insects hear with tympanal organs, which are like eardrums on their body's surface. These often pick up sounds of a certain pitch, helping insects to dodge particular predators and to locate potential mates.

Mouthparts detect ultrasonic sounds

Hawk moth
Some hawk moths have ears in their mouthparts. They use them to avoid attack by hunting bats.

Slit-shaped eardrum on forewing

Lacewing
Lacewings use their wing-mounted ears, like hawk moths, to detect the sounds of bats approaching.

Eardrum below middle joint of foreleg

Cricket
Crickets have eardrums on their front legs. These let them hear courtship calls of other crickets.

Eardrums underneath front of thorax

Tachinid fly
Using eardrums on their thorax, these parasitic flies often track down other insects by their calls.

Radiator ears

Compared to other animals, mammals often have eye-catching ears. The blacktailed jackrabbit's are some of the biggest relative to its body, measuring half its length from head to tail. They are very effective at collecting sound, but they are not only used for hearing. This jackrabbit lives in the deserts of western North America, where summer temperatures often climb above 104°F (40°C). Resting in the shade, it uses its ears like radiators to stop its body from overheating.

Network of blood vessels helps ears to radiate heat away from body

Full frontal

Like its body, an African elephant's ears are built on a giant scale. Elephants use them for hearing, keeping cool, and showing their mood. If they feel threatened, they spread them wide—a sign that they are ready to charge. Elephants communicate not only by trumpeting, but also with infrasound—sound so deep that humans cannot hear it. Infrasound waves travel through the ground as well as through the air.

Ear flap, or pinna, channels sound waves toward the eardrum, hidden inside the head

Eardrum on each side of abdomen

Cicada
The male cicada's ears are shaped in a way that keeps it from being deafened by its own piercing calls.

Inside ears

Swiveling on its head, the fennec fox's ears are alert to the faintest sounds. In addition to being big on the outside, its ears have an extra-large space shaped like a bubble, which separates the eardrum from the innermost part of the ear. This space works like an amplifier, helping sound waves to resonate. The fennec fox hunts after dark in the Sahara Desert and uses its ears to pinpoint insects and rodents as they scuttle across the ground.

Seeing with sound

When night falls, insect-eating bats take off from their daytime roosts and emerge to find food. Fluttering through the darkness on leathery wings, they catch prey in midair or snatch them from the ground. Unlike fruit-eating bats, they have tiny eyes, but they can swerve around all kinds of obstacles, from trees to phone lines, as they speed after their prey. The bats do this by using echolocation—a way of seeing their surroundings using rapid bursts of high-frequency sound. By listening for returning echoes, a bat builds up a picture of its world, including its food. Bats are not the only animals that use sound in this way. Several other kinds of mammal can echolocate, as can some birds that nest deep in caves.

Fly echoes

A hunting greater horseshoe bat squeaks with a constant pitch, or frequency. It distinguishes insect types by analyzing the echoes made by their beating wings. The echoes wobble in frequency due to Doppler shift, the effect that changes the pitch of a siren as it speeds past.

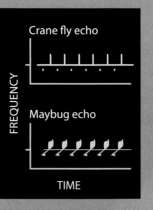

Crane fly echo

Maybug echo

FREQUENCY

TIME

Picture this

As it closes in on a moth, a greater horseshoe bat needs to know exactly how far away its prey is and how fast it is moving. It gives out more than 100 sound pulses a second—more than 20 times the rate when it is on patrol. It emits its sound pulses through its nostrils, in the center of its bizarre, horseshoe-shaped nose-leaf.

Ear swivels forward to collect echoes from moth

Nose-leaf's rounded shape focuses beam of outgoing sound

Ground sound

Aside from shrews, tenrecs are the only land-based mammals known to use echolocation. Living in Africa and Madagascar, they feed at night and make clicking sounds with their tongues as they move around. Unlike a bat's pulses, a tenrec's clicks can be heard by human ears.

Cave chorus

In Southeast Asia, cave swiftlets often roost and nest deep in limestone caves. They have good eyesight, but they use echolocation to find their way once they are underground. They make clicking sounds normally about 10 times a second, but in narrow passageways, the rate speeds up, giving the swiftlets a better picture of the route ahead.

Sound in the sea

Sound travels much better in water than it does in air, and it even penetrates the seabed. Ocean dolphins use it to find the echoes of flatfish hiding in the sand. They communicate with noisy whistles and squeaks, but their echolocation clicks can have a frequency of more than 150,000 Hz, which is far beyond the range of human hearing.

Phonic lips

Melon focuses outgoing sound waves

Blowhole

Fish in path of outgoing sound waves

Sound wave emitted by dolphin

Inner ear receives sound waves from jaw

Lower jaw collects returning echoes

Echo reflected by fish's swim bladder

Swim bladder

Dolphin clicks

Dolphins make click sounds with phonic lips—valves inside their heads, beneath their blowholes. They focus sound waves with the melon—a fatty pad that gives them a bulging forehead. Water lets sound pass, but a fish's gas-filled swim bladder reflects the sound, producing an echo.

Echoes in the deep

The sperm whale is the largest toothed whale and also the largest predator that hunts individual prey. It dives far into the sea's depths, where it uses sound to track down octopuses and squid. It produces the loudest and deepest echolocation clicks made by any animal, focusing them with spermaceti—a waxy substance that also adjusts the whale's buoyancy when diving.

Whale's enormous, square-fronted head is dominated by its spermaceti organ

Taste and smell

Unlike other senses, taste and smell work by detecting chemicals, often in incredibly small amounts. Animals use taste to identify food and to avoid harmful substances. Mammals taste with their taste buds, which are mainly on their tongues, but other animals taste with different body parts, or even their entire body surface. Smell detects substances that spread through air or water. Some odors warn of danger, but others are attractive, helping animals to find food or a potential mate.

Tasting the air

When exploring its surroundings, a rat snake constantly flicks its tongue in and out in order to collect chemicals from the air, which it analyzes in the roof of its mouth. Many snakes have forked tongues. They may use these to find the chemical's source, just as we use two ears to locate a sound. If the chemical is stronger on one tip than the other, this may guide a snake toward prey or away from a predator.

Jaws stay closed while tongue flicks in and out

Moist surface of tongue collects scent molecules from the air

Sensitive feet

This malachite butterfly is not simply perching on a leaf—it is tasting it as well. Butterflies can do this because they have taste sensors on their feet. This talent helps females to find the right plants to lay their eggs on, and it helps adults to track down food. Butterflies are especially attracted by sweet tastes. Their feet are more than 200 times as sensitive to sugar as human tongues.

Underwater smell

Orange cup corals cannot see their prey, but they are sensitive to movement and to waterborne chemicals given off by living things. If a fish swims nearby, the coral reacts to its scent and reaches for it with its stinging tentacles. In open water, many swimming predators use similar senses to track down their prey. Sharks are extremely good at detecting amino acids from injured flesh, smelling them even when they are diluted more than 10 billion times.

Jacobson's organ

After the snake flicks out its forked tongue, it presses the two tips into the nerved-lined opening of the Jacobson's organ in the roof of its mouth. Nerves in the organ sense the different chemicals that have been collected on the tongue and send signals to the brain. Some mammals also have a Jacobson's organ, which they use to detect pheromones—the airborne scents mammals use to communicate, particularly when they breed (see p. 137).

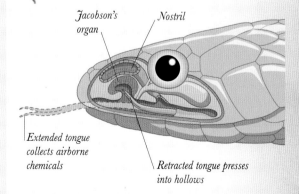

Jacobson's organ

Nostril

Extended tongue collects airborne chemicals

Retracted tongue presses into hollows

Best smellers

Male moths have some of the best chemical senses in the animal world. Males smell with their feathery antennae, which are specially "tuned in" to scent signals, or pheromones, produced by females that are ready to mate. Using its antennae, this male atlas moth can detect a female up to 6½ miles (11 km) away if it is upwind. The moth's antenna can sense minute changes in the strength of a pheromone trail. By zigzagging through the trail, the enormous moth—the world's biggest—eventually makes its way to the female.

Taste buds

With its rough surface, the tongue of an Arctic fox is just the right shape for tasting and manipulating food. Its roughness comes from small bumps called papillae. Some of these bumps have taste buds set in their surface. Shaped like microscopic barrels, taste buds have a collection of sensory hairs that react to food. Each taste bud senses a basic flavor, such as sour, salty, bitter, or sweet. The brain then puts them together to sense taste.

Large numbers of taste buds line trenches within papilla

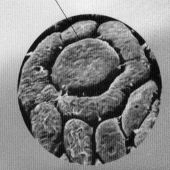

Magnified view of rounded papilla from back of tongue

Touch and motion

Animals use their sense of touch to feel their surroundings. If something new touches them, or moves nearby, they react right away. Animals use touch to protect themselves, to communicate, and also to find food. In addition to touch, animals have an internal sense that detects gravity and motion, telling them which way up they are.

Touchy feeders

Giant anteaters have very poor eyesight and track down their food by smell. Once they have found an ant or termite nest, they use touch to help gather up their food. A giant anteater's tongue can be up to 20 in (50 cm) long, and its sensitive tip probes deep inside a nest's narrow galleries. Using a large amount of sticky saliva that works like glue, the tongue flicks in and out like a high-speed pump, collecting up to 25,000 insects a day.

Statocyst located near base of first pair of antennae

Feelings inside

Animals need to be able to tell up from down. A crab does this with its eyes and, like most invertebrates, also with internal sensors called statocysts. A statocyst is a hollow chamber containing a heavy mineral grain. Gravity pulls the grain, triggering the statocyst. This tells the crab which way is up and whether it is speeding up or slowing down. Vertebrates have similar sense organs in their inner ear.

Toothless jaws form a tubular snout

Powerful claw, which folds back when walking, rips open an insect nest

Long, narrow tongue

Guard hair detects contact or movement in water or air

Wool, or underfur

Touch receptor near skin's surface senses light touch

Pressure receptor deep in skin

Erector muscle contracts causing guard hair to stand on end

Sebaceous gland secretes wax that lubricates skin and hair

Nerve ending wrapped around follicle of guard hair

Sensitive feet rest on water's surface film, waiting for ripples

Stabbing mouthparts fold away against body when not in use

Fatal vibrations

Hanging upside down at the surface of a pond, a backswimmer uses ripples to find its prey. It ignores powerful splashes, but is attracted by small, rapid ripples—the kind produced when insects fall into the water and struggle to escape. It rows toward their source and attacks its prey from underneath, stabbing it with its tubelike mouthparts. Backswimmers are aggressive predators and often fight each other for a share of the food.

Synchronized swimmers

When fish swim in a shoal, they move in a coordinated way by using a special pressure-sensing system. Called a lateral line, it keeps these catfish tightly together, making it hard for predators to single out their prey. A fish has two lateral lines—one along each side. Each one consists of a fluid-filled tube connected to the outside by small holes, or pores. Inside the tube is a row of sensors that detect pressure waves. When a fish moves, its neighbors sense the movement with their lateral lines. Within a split second, they move, too.

Skin, hair, and whiskers

Swimming mammals, such as otters, often rely on their sense of touch when they hunt. Otters use their whiskers to find food in murky water and to hunt after dark. Their paws are also very sensitive. They feel for food or hold it down when the otter eats. At sea, seals and walruses also use their whiskers to find food. A walrus has up to 700 whiskers on its upper lip. Together, they form a bristly "moustache" up to 12 in (30 cm) long.

Muzzle contains highest concentration of touch sensors, along with paws

Wired up

Mammals sense touch and pressure with specialized nerve endings, which are set at different depths in their skin. If anything touches the surface of their fur, it makes guard hairs move, which triggers nerves that are wrapped around their roots. Whiskers are even more sensitive. They grow in specialized follicles, and signals from them are processed by a particular part of the brain.

Spreading whiskers sense objects across a wide area

Star performer

The star-nosed mole of North America is a hunter with an incredibly good sense of touch. It can barely see, but it can feel the tiniest soil animals using a ring of 22 fleshy tentacles around its nostrils. With a total of 25,000 tiny touch sensors, the tentacles are more sensitive than human fingertips, and they constantly wriggle, testing the soil for food. If a tentacle touches something promising, the mole quickly feels it with the lowest pair, which are the most sensitive of all. It can identify food and swallow it in just 0.25 seconds, making it one of the fastest-eating mammals in the world.

125

Special senses

Many animals sense things that we cannot and that are hard for us to imagine. On land, some snakes "see" infrared radiation, which lets them hunt warm-blooded animals after dark. In water, platypuses and sharks sense the faint electric fields produced by their prey—using a special sense known as electroreception. But special senses are not used only to find food. A wide variety of animals, including turtles, birds, and bats, can sense the strength and direction of Earth's magnetic field. When they migrate, their magnetic sense can help to guide them to their destination.

Electric inspection

The platypus's rubbery bill is highly sensitive to touch, but it also has around 40,000 tiny sensors that detect electric fields. When the platypus is hunting, it sweeps its bill from side to side, which lets it sense the electric fields of small animals buried in the riverbed mud. Once it has found the food, it uses its bill to dig it out quickly.

Sensing heat

All warm objects give off infrared radiation—a form of energy that carries heat. Rattlesnakes, pythons, and boas can detect it at extremely low levels, through heat-sensitive pits in their faces. Using its pits, this green tree python can strike mammals or birds in total darkness, as long as they are against a colder background. Rattlesnakes have two pits, but pythons and boas have several along the sides of their mouths.

Sensory signals from eye are processed by same part of brain as signals from pits

Wedge-shaped pit lined with heat-sensitive nerves

Electroreception

Some fish can produce massive electric shocks, which they use to stun or kill their prey. Many more fish, such as sharks and rays, sense the electric fields created by other fish. A shark does this with gel-filled sensors, or ampullae, clustered in its head. It can detect differences of a millionth of a volt, guiding the shark toward the source of the field.

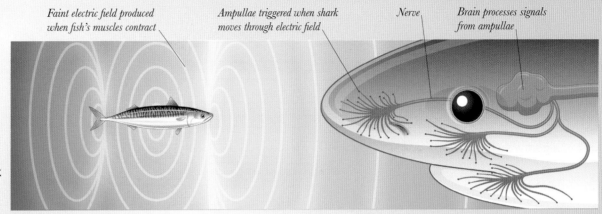

Faint electric field produced when fish's muscles contract

Ampullae triggered when shark moves through electric field

Nerve

Brain processes signals from ampullae

Magnetic compass

When green turtles breed, they usually head back to the beaches where they were born, sometimes traveling vast distances. Like migrating birds, the turtles navigate in several ways. In addition to steering by looking at the Sun and stars, they may be guided by crystals of magnetite—an iron-based mineral in their brains. Magnetite is the most magnetic natural mineral on Earth and is found in many animals that steer by Earth's magnetic field.

Magnified view of a magnetite crystal

Feeling pressured

Animals cannot forecast the weather, but many can sense changes in air pressure. A gradual rise usually means the weather is becoming drier and more settled, while a sudden drop means stormy weather may be on its way. Swifts often travel away from low pressure air, returning when the pressure rises again.

Magnetic architects

In Australia, magnetic termites build slab-shaped nests with narrow edges pointing north and south. As the Sun travels east to west, there is always one face in shadow where termites can keep cool, and at noon, only the top edge is exposed to direct sunlight. Worker termites are blind, so they cannot use the Sun as a guide to line up their nests. Instead, they sense Earth's magnetic field.

Keeping in contact

Signaling by sight

Communication is a key part of life—not just for humans, but for most wild animals, too. Keeping in contact helps animals to survive and to breed. Animals usually signal to their own kind, but messages sometimes pass between different species, particularly when one is threatening another with attack. Animal signals range from physical contact when animals meet, to beautiful and complex songs from birds and whales. But for many animals, the most important way of signaling is by sight. Using colors, movements, or facial expressions, they make sure that they get their message across.

Lines of communication

Communication and senses are closely linked. Some animals can communicate by sensing vibrations or electric fields, but most send and receive signals by touch, sight, sound, or smell. Each species communicates in private by coding its signals as particular calls or scents, which helps to stop predators from homing in.

Touch
For lovebirds, touch is a way of maintaining bonds, especially between partners and between parents and their young. Animals also use touch when grooming.

Sight
With bright warning colors and its fins spread, a lion fish gives out a visual message that it has poisonous spines. Visual messages work both within and between species.

Sound
Coyotes howl to keep in touch with each other. Sound signals work on land and in water and let animals communicate even when they cannot be seen.

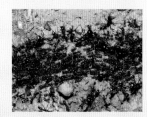

Smell
Driver ants follow trails by sensing a scent, or pheromone. Unlike sound, chemical messages can be long-lasting, because many pheromones take time to fade away.

Body language

Cowering in the snow with its ears back, a gray wolf gives way to a more dominant wolf in its pack. Its behavior is an example of body language—a kind of visual signaling found throughout the animal world. Many animals use body language with their own kind, but it can also be a lifesaver in emergencies, by making animals look bigger or more dangerous than they really are.

Mottled plumage helps female blend in with nest site on rocky ground

Male king eider duck

Spot the difference

Colors and patterns often work like an identity badge. Here, a female king eider is flanked by two males, wearing their eye-catching breeding plumage. Male ducks dress to impress, because it helps them to attract mates. They often grow their bright plumage just before the breeding season begins. Female ducks are the opposite. Most of them have camouflaged plumage, which helps them to hide while they are sitting on their eggs.

Scare tactics

With its plump body, the eyed hawk moth is a tempting meal for hungry birds. The moth is well camouflaged, but if it is spotted, it has a way of fighting for its life. It suddenly opens up its wings and reveals markings that look like a pair of large, staring eyes. If luck is on its side, the bird hesitates and moves on. This kind of visual trickery is common in insects, and it is also used by some bigger animals, including fish and frogs.

Wing opens to reveal "eye"

Closed wings are well camouflaged

Making faces

Most animals cannot make faces because they have little or no muscle to make their faces move. Mammals are different. Some kinds—particularly monkeys and apes—can make a wide range of facial expressions. Their expressions may look like ours, but their meaning isn't always the same. This chimp is making a face called a pout. This is often used as a sign of submission after a fight, but in young chimps it can be a way of begging for food.

Watch this

Male fiddler crabs live in burrows in mangrove swamps and come out to feed at low tide. Although they are small—often just 1 in (2.5 cm) across—they have one giant claw that they use to signal across the mud. A fiddler crab extends its claw as though it is beckoning and then suddenly flicks it back. This display attracts females and warns rival males away. There are many species of fiddler crab. Each kind has its own signal pattern, so females can find the right type of mate.

Flashing lights

On warm nights, fireflies attract partners by flashing a built-in light. The light is produced on their undersides by a chemical reaction that gives off a yellow or green glow, but almost no heat. The males flash on and off as they fly through the dark. Females flash back, and the males land next to them to mate. Each species has its own coded sequence of flashes, and in some kinds, all the males flash in step.

Back off!

Some animal signals are difficult to interpret, but there is no mistaking this cheetah's snarl as it tries to defend its kill. From the moment it brings down its prey, the cheetah is on guard, because scavengers and predators will be attracted by the prospect of food. Cheetahs are superb sprinters, but they are not so good at fending off other predators. Females with cubs often put up a fight against hyenas, but if lions appear in the distance, a cheetah will abandon its meal and run away.

Calls and songs

Nature's airwaves are crowded with animal sounds, and so are the oceans and seas. Small animals can be surprisingly loud, and whale songs can reach more than 180 decibels—even louder than a passenger jet. Many animals make sounds by breathing out so that the air vibrates, but some insects rub body parts together or click membranes that work like tiny high-pitched drums. Sounds help animals to attract a mate and let them keep in touch, sometimes over astounding distances. Sounds can also keep danger at bay. In emergencies, a warning hiss can stop a predator in its tracks.

Practice makes perfect

A sedge wren weighs less than ½ oz (10 g), but its chattering song carries a long way in still air. Like all songbirds, it has a well-developed voicebox, or syrinx, deep inside its chest. The syrinx contains a complex set of muscles and membranes, which tighten and relax to produce a fast-changing stream of notes. Male wrens are born with the instinct to sing, but they learn their song by listening to and copying the older males.

One among many

Northern gannets nest in densely packed colonies containing up to 50,000 breeding pairs and their young. Amazingly, they use sound to recognize one another, despite the clamor of all the other birds and the background noise of the wind and the waves. Adults honk as they come in to land, and their partners need less than a second to identify them. They call back, guiding their partner to touch down in the right place.

Outside broadcast

In spring and summer, male green tree frogs croak to attract a mate. They have vocal cords, like we do, but they also have a vocal sac, which works like an inflatable amplifier. To start calling, a frog breathes in and then closes its nostrils. It forces the air backward and forward between its lungs and vocal sac, so that its vocal cords can make the air vibrate. Green tree frogs have a single sac, but many other frogs have one on each side of their heads.

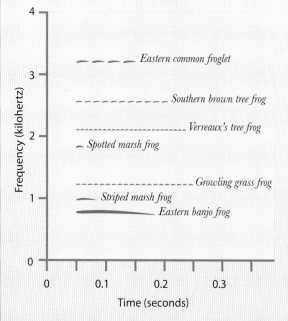

Air resonates inside vocal sac, amplifying frog's call

Private audience

The males of each species of frog have their own distinctive call, making sure that they attract females of the right species. This is particularly important when several species breed in the same place. The calls of seven Australian frogs are shown on this graph. They often use the same pools to breed in and call at the same time of day, but each call has its own frequency, or pitch, and its own rhythm and timing.

Graph — Frequency (kilohertz) vs Time (seconds)

- Eastern common froglet
- Southern brown tree frog
- Verreaux's tree frog
- Spotted marsh frog
- Growling grass frog
- Striped marsh frog
- Eastern banjo frog

Frequency (kilohertz): 0, 1, 2, 3, 4
Time (seconds): 0, 0.1, 0.2, 0.3

Songs beneath the sea

Filled with deep rumbles, creaking sounds, and squeaks, the humpback whale's song is one of the longest and eeriest in the animal world. A complete song can last for more than 15 minutes and contains separate themes and phrases that slowly change over a period of years. Only the males sing, and whales in the same social group sing the same song, with the same variations, even if they are thousands of miles apart. No one knows exactly why whales sing. The most likely explanation is that it helps males to attract potential mates.

Treetop chorus

Leaf-eating howler monkeys are among the world's loudest land animals. They live in tropical forests and use their roaring calls to signal to neighboring troops up to 3 miles (5 km) away. The chorus warns the neighbors to keep their distance and not to compete with the troop for food. In their throats, howlers have an extra-large hyoid bone. Shaped like a bowl, it makes sound reverberate when they call.

Flight feathers reverberate when wings are flicked together

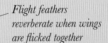

Insect sounds

Insects do not have lungs, so they cannot make sounds by breathing. Instead, many kinds chirp or sing by rubbing one body part against another—a technique called stridulation. Most grasshoppers, such as this one, rub their hind legs against their forewings. Their hind legs have a row of small pegs, which scrape against the wings to make sound. Crickets sing in a slightly different way, by rubbing one forewing against the other.

Inner surface of grasshopper's hind leg rubs against thickened forewing

Bird musicians

In addition to singing, birds communicate in other ways. Woodpeckers signal by hammering on tree trunks, while many birds clatter their beaks, or clap their wingtips together when they fly. Some of the strangest sounds are made by club-winged manakins. Males have special wing feathers with large, hollow shafts. They flick these together over their backs, making a sound like a wheezy violin.

Signals in scent

The living world is full of chemical signals, which we rarely notice. Produced by animals, many are dedicated scent chemicals called pheromones, which work like invisible control systems, affecting the way their own kind develop or behave. There are many types of pheromone, and they are often produced in microscopic amounts. Even so, their effects can be dramatic. Pheromones are used to mark territory, ward off danger, indicate when a female is ready to breed, and help a mother identify her young. They are particularly important for insects and other invertebrates, and for mammals with a better sense of smell than our own.

Male plains zebra

Calling card

While its baby clings to its back, a female ring-tailed lemur leaves a scent mark from her anal gland, just beneath her tail. Scent marking is very common in mammals. Hoofed mammals have scent glands on their feet, and others near their eyes, which they use for marking grass or twigs. By leaving their scent, mammals show others of their kind when they last passed by. Males use scent to claim territories and to warn rivals to keep away.

Female Thomson's gazelle sniffs her newborn calf

Potty trained

Domestic cats are careful to bury their droppings, but many other mammals leave theirs in conspicuous heaps, known as latrines. This European river otter is depositing its droppings, or spraint, to mark its territory. A male's territory can extend over 6 miles (10 km) of riverbanks or coasts. Inside its boundaries, the otter maintains dozens of latrine sites, showing other males that they are intruding on private ground.

Otter droppings mark its territory

Something in the air

Curling back its upper lip, this male zebra is testing the air around the hind quarters of a female for pheromones. This behavior, called flehmen, passes air over the Jacobson's organ, which is in the roof of its mouth (see p. 120). This organ detects pheromones in tiny amounts, letting the zebra know if the female is ready to breed.

Secret signals

Insects use pheromones throughout their lives. Some kinds—such as alarm pheromones—produce sudden changes in behavior. Others work more slowly, affecting the way insects grow and develop. Queen bees release slow-acting pheromones to control their workers and to keep their nests running smoothly.

Sex pheromones
Powerful attractants called sex pheromones bring males and females together so that they can mate. In grasshoppers—and most other insects—the female produces the pheromone, guiding the male toward her.

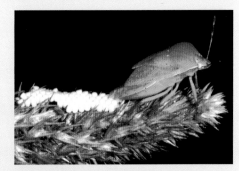

Spacing pheromones
Like many other insects, plant bugs leave spacing pheromones when they lay their eggs. These pheromones "tag" plants that have eggs, so that other females do not lay theirs in the same place.

Trail pheromones
Processionary moth caterpillars live in silk nests in trees. When they emerge to feed, they move in formation, laying down a trail pheromone. This later guides them back to their nest.

Alarm pheromones
If honeybees are attacked or injured, they release an alarm pheromone, which makes other bees go on the attack. These bees also give off the pheromone, so thousands soon join in.

Smells familiar

Minutes after being born on Africa's grassy plains, a young Thomson's gazelle is helped to its feet by its mother. As she licks her calf, she memorizes its scent, helping her to identify it until it is old enough to fend for itself. From this moment onward, she feeds her calf on her milk, but will push away any "foreign-smelling" calves.

Stink bombs

In addition to making pheromones, many insects use chemicals for self-defense. Threatened by a predator, this swallowtail caterpillar has inflated a gland called an osmeterium, which is shaped like a pair of miniature horns. It not only looks alarming, but it also gives off a powerful smell. Beetles and plant-sucking bugs are also expert at this kind of chemical warfare. Bombardier beetles produce an evil-smelling explosive spray that squirts out of their abdomens with a loud pop.

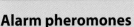

Osmeterium extends to form a pair of horn-shaped scent weapons

Swallowtail caterpillar

Staying in touch

Touch works only at close range, but it plays a big part in animal communication. Animals often use it when they meet and when they are getting together to mate. In mammals and birds, it helps parents to control their young, as well as to maintain the bonds between parents themselves. Touch is even more important for animals that live in permanent groups. They often spend hours in close contact, exchanging signals by touch.

Touching moment

Despite its size, an elephant's trunk is almost as sensitive as a human hand. Here, two African elephants are meeting and greeting. One has laid its trunk on the other's head and is smelling its temporal gland, just in front of its ear. This gland produces a mixture of chemicals, which give the elephant a complex personal scent. After even a short separation, related elephants greet by touching and rubbing with their trunks, to reconfirm their close connections.

Personal space

Perched on nests made of mud, black-browed albatross chicks wait patiently for their parents to return from the ocean with food. Each nest is surrounded by a personal "buffer zone," which stretches as far as an adult albatross can peck. The parents can come and go, but they attack any other albatross that ventures too close to their nest.

Getting up close

For African meerkats, keeping in touch is an essential part of life. Meerkats live in groups, or packs, in southern Africa's dry, sandy plains. They huddle together in the early morning sunshine to groom and to build social bonds, and they spend the nights close up, in burrows underground. When the adults go out hunting, helpful "aunts" look after the young that are left behind.

Head-to-head meeting

When two ants meet, they often touch each other with their antennae and their mouths. The contact lasts for just a split second, but it is long enough for them to exchange food and pheromones. A single worker may meet other ants thousands of times a day, so this communication system can quickly spread signals—and food—throughout the nest.

Dances in the dark

Honeybees use touch in a remarkable way to tell others where to find food. Returning scouts carry out dances inside the dark hive, and other bees feel the air movement. The way a scout waggles its body, walks in circles, and vibrates its wings tells them the distance to the flowers and their direction relative to the Sun.

Sun

Waggle direction indicates angle of nectar source to the Sun

Nectar source is at this angle to the Sun

Workers follow directions to nectar source

Nectar source

Hive

Teaming up

Sometimes, animals from different species communicate so that they can work together as a team. The watchman goby shares a burrow excavated by the pistol shrimp. If danger threatens, the goby warns the nearly blind shrimp by touching it with its tail, and the two retreat into their shared home.

Shrimp uses antenna to communicate by touch with goby

Attracting a mate

When the breeding season arrives, animals concentrate on the all-important task of finding a mate. For males, competition for partners can be fierce, and many species put all their energy into showing off or into fighting with rival males. Zebras bite and kick, while kangaroos trade kicks and punches, but many contests are set-piece rituals where the loser escapes unharmed. In some species, males gather at "showgrounds" called leks, where they compete for center stage and the chance to mate with the most females. Females rarely fight over males. Instead, they do the choosing. They look for partners that are strong and healthy, with the best territories, or with the most eye-catching displays.

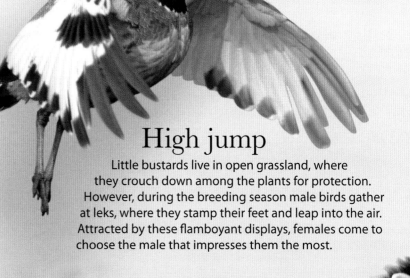

Neck feathers are fluffed out during display

High jump

Little bustards live in open grassland, where they crouch down among the plants for protection. However, during the breeding season male birds gather at leks, where they stamp their feet and leap into the air. Attracted by these flamboyant displays, females come to choose the male that impresses them the most.

Battle for supremacy

On the edge of a waterhole, a plains zebra delivers a painful bite to a rival's neck. When males fight, a well-aimed kick is most dangerous, particularly if it lands on the opponent's legs—a lame zebra is soon picked off by predators. The strongest breeding males control a group, or harem, of up to six females. The harem stays together along with any young, even when they form part of a bigger herd.

Arching wall of bower up to 18 in (45 cm) high

The art of attraction

Male bowerbirds appeal to females by building bizarre structures called bowers, which contain hundreds of carefully arranged sticks. Here, a male great bowerbird is using shells to decorate a completed bower. His handiwork has already attracted a female, who is inspecting the bower from inside. After mating, the female flies away and builds herself a nest.

Fancy dress

With their fan-shaped crests and brilliant orange plumage, male Guianan cocks-of-the-rock put on a spectacular show. During the breeding season, they strut, jump, and squawk at their lek on the forest floor. They sometimes clash head-on, furiously flapping their wings. Females come to choose a male and mate. Then, they fly off to raise their family elsewhere.

Claiming a territory

Some animal territories are used only for mating, but they still need enough space and food for a growing family. This male tree frog has claimed one of the tiniest territories imaginable—a pool of rainwater in the leaves of a bromeliad plant. The male attracts a female with his mating call. The female then lays her eggs in the pool, high up in the rain forest canopy.

Rival male loses challenge by suffering a wound to the neck

Ritual combat

Many animals avoid violent fights by holding ritual combats to decide which male gets the upper hand. During these contests, the stronger male asserts his supremacy and the loser gets a chance to back down.

Twisting adders

Rival male adders twist together as they crawl across the ground. They rear up and press against one another over and over again, until one of the snakes gives in.

Wrestling frogs

Poison dart frogs are highly territorial. Males fight off intruders by winning wrestling matches, where the frogs grapple with their front legs. Females also wrestle to win the best nesting sites.

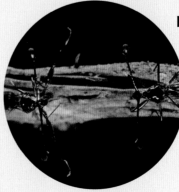

Fly standoff

Male stalk-eyed flies have eyes at the end of extremely slender stalks. When two males meet, they stand face to face and size each other up. The fly with the longest eye stalks wins the contest.

Courtship gift

For European bee-eaters, the bond between male and female is often sealed with gifts of food. Here, a male offers his partner a butterfly, which he has caught in midair. His behavior is partly triggered by the female. She begs for food by opening her beak and fluttering her wings—behavior that imitates a young bird. During their courtship, the male presents the female with dozens of meals a day, giving her the energy she needs for making and laying her eggs.

Pairing up

Mating is a crucial moment in animals' lives, because it is the start of the next generation. But before two animals pair up, they need to get over their natural wariness of each other. Animals do this by carrying out courtship rituals, which bond them together like players on a team. Once the bond has been formed, the partners can breed. In most water animals, the male fertilizes the female's eggs once they have been laid. In land animals, the male usually mates with the female, so that his sperm fertilizes her eggs inside her body. She then lays the eggs or gives birth to live young.

Dicing with death

A male golden orb web spider approaches a female, which is many times his own size, very cautiously. He announces his arrival by tugging on the web using signals that work like a code. If all goes well, this stops her from treating him as a meal. If she attacks, he nimbly jumps off the web using a silk line to lower himself to safety.

Male grips female with set of claspers at end of abdomen

Internal mating

When butterflies mate, they face in opposite directions with their abdomens locked together. These two blue butterflies may stay like this for more than an hour while the male (on the left) transfers his sperm. Inside the female, the sperm is held in a special storage pouch until her eggs are ready to be fertilized.

Come dancing

Many birds perform courtship dances. Some are short and simple, but the great crested grebe's is amazingly complex. The two partners dance on the surface of a lake, and the complete performance involves several linked dances and displays. Each partner has to follow exactly the right steps. If all goes well, the pair forms a bond, and the female allows the male to mate.

Head-shaking dance
In the early stages of courtship, the partners swim up to each other, coming face to face. They wag their heads, pointing their bills up and down.

Dive and rush
Both birds dive to the bottom of the lake and grab a piece of weed. They bring it up to the surface and rush toward each other at high speed.

Weed ceremony
Paddling as hard as they can, the two birds rear up out of the water, presenting each other with the weed that they have collected.

Partners in slime

Great gray slugs are both male and female at the same time. But instead of fertilizing themselves, they need to find a partner, and then lower themselves from a long thread of slime. Next, the two slugs extend their reproductive organs, which look like umbrellas. They fertilize each other, and then crawl away to lay their eggs.

Broody pair

Swimming upside down, a male clownfish fertilizes his partner's bright orange eggs by squirting sperm onto them while they are glued to a rock. This way of breeding is called external fertilization, because it occurs outside the female's body. Once the eggs have been fertilized, the male clownfish takes charge of them until they hatch. He fans water over them with his fin and chases away egg-eating predators.

Entwined penises exchange sperm, so that each slug's eggs are fertilized

End of the affair

Some animal partnerships come to a quick and gruesome end. This female praying mantis has mated with a male and has started to eat him, beginning with his head. Despite losing his head, the male continues to fertilize the female, and his body provides her with a useful meal. Not all male mantises share this chilling fate—some manage to mate and then escape.

Animal families

Starting life

Most animals start life as a fertilized egg made up of a single cell. Eggs are often microscopic and not all of them have shells, but from this simple beginning the original cell divides many times. Gradually, a new individual called an embryo starts to take shape. In mammals, embryos usually develop inside the mother's body until the young are ready to be born. For many other animals, life really gets underway with hatching, when a new animal emerges from its egg into the outside world.

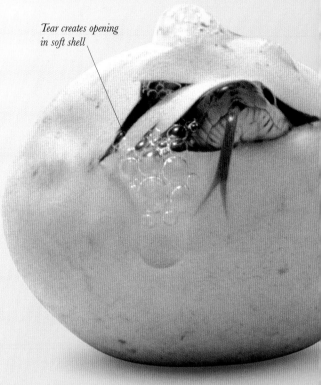

Tear creates opening in soft shell

Snake first uses its egg tooth to cut several slices in the shell

Growth sac

Many sharks and rays lay pouch-shaped eggs with tough, fibrous cases. This egg was laid by a Japanese swell shark that lives near coasts in the Pacific Ocean. The case has tendrils at its corners, which anchor the egg to seaweed while the fish embryo develops inside, taking nourishment from the yolk sac.

Yolk sac supplies developing shark with nutrients

Lone breakout

Some snakes give birth to live young, but rat snakes lay eggs with leathery shells. About 10 weeks after the eggs are laid, the young snakes hatch. They use a pointed scale on the tip of their upper jaw called an egg tooth to slice their way through the shell. Unlike mammals or birds, these reptiles are not looked after by their parents. From the moment they hatch, the rat snakes have to fend for themselves.

How embryos develop

A chick starts life even before the egg is laid by the hen. The single cell divides to form a hollow disk lying on the yolk sac. In the days after the egg is laid, the disk starts to form different organs and the chick's heart begins to beat. The embryo develops rapidly, using up the food stored in the yolk. After three weeks, the chick is ready to hatch.

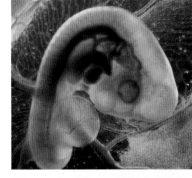

Microscopic embryo
Day 3—the head, eyes, and leg buds form. The heart pumps blood containing food and oxygen to the developing cells.

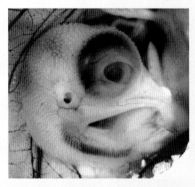

Growing body
Day 9—the embryo is still featherless, but has a large head and legs. The yolk sac shrinks as the chick's body grows.

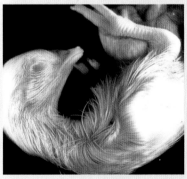

Fully formed chick
Day 19—with just 48 hours to go until hatching, the chick now has feathers, wings, and well-developed legs.

Forked tongue tastes and smells the outside world

Single parent

This female aphid is giving birth, without having mated first. This way of breeding is quite common in insects. In spring, when food is plentiful, some female aphids can produce up to 10 young a day. Each one is a tiny copy, or clone, of the mother. Male and female aphids also mate later in the year to produce eggs, which can survive through the winter months.

Once the shell has been torn open, the snake may stay inside its egg for several more hours

Finally, the tiny rat snake slides out of the egg, leaving its crumpled shell behind

Hungry hatchling

Even when they are tiny, caterpillars have strong jaws. This owl butterfly caterpillar has just chewed its way out of its egg and is setting off in search of food. Many caterpillars eat their shells after hatching. The shells are rich in protein, so they make a nutritious first meal.

Giving birth

Watched anxiously by its mother, a young guanaco makes its entrance into the world. Some mammals—including guanacos—give birth to young that can walk and run within a few hours. At the other extreme, newly born pouched mammals, or marsupials—such as kangaroos—are tiny, hairless, and blind. To survive, they must continue growing inside their mother's pouch.

Amorous amphibians

As the breeding season nears its end, several male European common frogs wait for females in the shallow water of a pond. The frogs are dwarfed by mounds of jelly-covered eggs, or spawn, which other females have already laid in the water. A single female can produce up to 4,000 eggs at a time and these are fertilized externally by a male clinging to her back. At first, the eggs are small, but their clear, jellylike coating absorbs water and swells up, protecting the embryos developing inside. The tadpoles, or frog larvae, take about a month to hatch.

Changing shape

All animals change size and shape as they grow up. In some animals, however, the young and adults look completely different and live in different ways. The transformation from young to adult often happens gradually in a process called metamorphosis—for example, when a tadpole turns into a newt or a frog. But for other animals, including butterflies, metamorphosis is a single dramatic event. The animal's entire body breaks down into a soup, and a new body forms in its place.

Chrysalis shell remains in place after butterfly climbs out

Wings expand and harden as blood pumps through them

Adult painted lady pulls itself free of the chrysalis case

Complete transformation

Like all butterflies, the painted lady undergoes an amazing transformation called complete metamorphosis. It starts its life as a crawling caterpillar, which feeds hungrily on leaves for about four weeks. Next, the caterpillar attaches itself to a stem and spins a silk case called a chrysalis. Inside the chrysalis, the caterpillar's body is first liquefied, and then the cells reorganize themselves in the new shape of a butterfly. Finally, the chrysalis splits open and the adult butterfly emerges with crumpled wings.

Caterpillar hangs upside down to spin its chrysalis

Caterpillar's body changes inside the hanging chrysalis

Right side up

Flatfish, such as this flounder, start life swimming in open water with an eye on each side of their heads, just like other fish. As the fish grow, their bodies flatten out and they lie on one side, partially buried on the seabed. Over time, the eye that was facing downward gradually creeps across the fish's head, forming a mismatched pair on the upper side of its body.

Change of skin

Some insects change shape gradually, each time they shed their "exoskeleton" body case. Their wings develop from small buds, and so only the adults can fly. This bush cricket is finishing its final molt. Its old exoskeleton has split open and the adult insect climbs out with fully formed wings, ready to breed. This growing process is called gradual, or incomplete, metamorphosis, because the changes are small. Dragonflies and cockroaches also develop in this way.

Abandoned exoskeleton remains hanging from foliage

Young adrift

Metamorphosis is very common among sea animals and many invertebrates have young, or larvae, that drift with the currents. Over the weeks or months, the larvae slowly grow and change shape. They often settle on the shore or seabed before becoming adults.

Barnacle larva
This newly hatched barnacle larva has a single eye. It swims and feeds by using its feathery antennae.

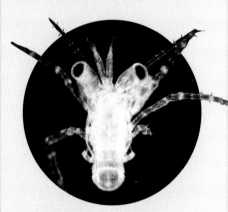

Crab larva
Halfway to adulthood, this crab larva has large eyes and strong legs. It lives and feeds on the seabed.

Eye not yet fully formed

14-day-old tadpole leaves jelly

12-day-old embryo

From water to land

Great crested newts lay their eggs in ponds. Their newly hatched tadpoles are tiny and almost transparent, with feathery gills and no trace of any legs. During the following four months, the tadpoles grow up fast and their bodies transform. Their gills shrink and they develop lungs and spindly legs. The fully grown newts can breathe with their lungs as well as through their skin, ready for life on land and in the water. Several years then pass before the adult newts are old enough to breed.

Egg in jellylike case

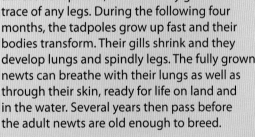

Spindly leg not yet ready for walking on land

External gills allow breathing in water

28-day-old tadpole grows legs

Male adult newt returns to pond to breed

Five toes on hind leg

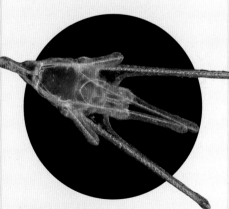

Sea urchin larva
Long arms, reinforced by hard mineral spikes, help this sea urchin larva to drift near the surface of the ocean.

Building a home

The animal world includes some amazingly gifted builders. They make homes to protect themselves and, even more importantly, to shelter their young. Some animal homes could fit in a thimble, but the largest can be taller than a house and take generations to construct and maintain. All animals rely on inborn behavior called instinct to help them assemble a new home using the right building materials.

Stately piles

Many birds build a new nest each spring to house their eggs and chicks, but bald eagle pairs reuse the same one for up to 20 years. Both partners help to repair their old nest high up in a tree by adding fresh supplies of sticks. After many years of construction, a bald eagle nest can be enormous. One of the largest ever found measured 20 ft (6 m) from top to bottom—as tall as a two-story house—and weighed nearly a ton.

Beaver lodges

Beavers build the largest structures in the animal world, aside from coral reefs. They cut down trees and branches and use stones and mud to construct dams across rivers and streams. Some beaver dams are more than 1,600 ft (500 m) long. These create a pond that surrounds and protects their family living quarters, or lodge, which is built from a huge pile of sticks.

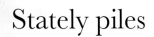

Lodge roof covered with sticks and sealed with mud

Sleeping chamber above water

Underwater passage

Heavy stones brace dam

Beaver packs mud to seal dam

Nest hangs from thin tree branch as protection against predators

Mobile home

Some animals make portable homes just for themselves. This cluster of tiny sticks is a case made by a bagworm—a moth caterpillar that feeds on leaves. The sticks are fastened together with silk, and they camouflage the caterpillar from insect-eating birds. Males eventually emerge from their cases to mate, but females often stay inside all their lives.

Plant material disguises silk bag containing bagworm

Show home

Hanging upside down, a male southern masked weaver uses his bill to stitch another blade of grass into his nest. Male birds do all the building work—first, collecting strips of flexible, green grass and then weaving and knotting them into a hollow, hanging ball. The birds become more skilled at constructing their woven nests each time they build. Once finished, the bird hangs beneath the nest and flutters his wings, inviting females to mate and move in.

Woven grass strips form domed nest chamber

Burrow entrance

Nest made of grass and fur

Underground maze

Many insects dig burrows, but the largest tunnels are made by mammals. European rabbit colonies live in a warren—a network of burrows that can have many entrances and more than 800 ft (250 m) of tunnels. The rabbits graze in the open, but they rarely stray far from the warren. At the first sign of danger, they disappear to safety underground.

Building materials

Animals build their homes with the materials they find in their local habitat and many use them in their natural form. Some animals, however, shape or process their materials first—perhaps by chewing them, or by mixing them with spit, or saliva. Other animals can produce building materials, such as spider's silk or beeswax, with their own bodies.

Leaves
Australian green ants make bag-shaped nests from folded leaves. Chains of ants pull the leaves into position, and then glue them together with the sticky silk that is produced by their grubs.

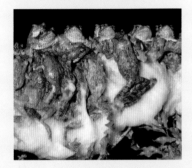

Foam
Foam-nest frogs whip up their own mucus to make hanging nests for their eggs in trees. Once the tadpoles develop in the foam, they wriggle out of the nest and drop into pools and streams.

Clay
Some termites build their nests from wood fibers, but the largest mounds are made from particles of clay mixed with saliva. They tower up to 30 ft (9 m) high and have deep, underground passages.

Grass
The tiny harvest mouse collects blades of grass, which it shreds and uses to weave a ball-shaped nest. The nest is attached to grass stems about 1 ft (30 cm) above the ground.

Wood fibers
Common wasps use their jaws to chew up dead wood fibers and mix them with saliva to form a paste. The wasps spread out the paste in sheets, which dry to form the paper walls of their nest.

Parental care

Many young animals never see their parents. Instead, they have to look after themselves. But for others, life gets off to a much safer start, thanks to caring parents. These parents protect their young from predators, and often lead their young to food. Some parents go even further, by collecting food for their offspring, or by making it themselves. Usually it is the female that does the caring, or both parents working as a team. But in some animals, such as ostriches and mouthbrooding fish, the male raises the family on his own.

Follow the leader

Once young ostriches have left their nest, they follow their father, who teaches them where to feed. When different families meet, they often join together to form a giant family, or crèche. A crèche can contain more than 50 chicks supervised by a dominant male.

Newly hatched crocodile carried from nest to water

Gentle jaws

Despite their fearsome teeth, female crocodiles are remarkably gentle parents. They bury their eggs in riverside nests and wait nearby for nearly three months until the young are ready to hatch. As soon as the young start to squeak, the mother digs down to the nest and carries the babies to water in her jaws. Instinct prevents her from closing her mouth, so her young are safe.

Full back

Life is a race for young Virginia opossums, because their mother gives birth to more young than she has teats. The strongest, fastest babies find her pouch first and fasten themselves onto a spare teat, where they drink her milk. Once they are around two months old, they leave her pouch and she carries them around on her back.

Guard duty

In the insect world, caring parents are rare. This plant bug is an exception. She guards her clutch of eggs around the clock. Once her young have hatched, she stays with them until they have shed their cases, or exoskeletons, for the first time. After that, the young bugs are on their own.

Eggs glued in tight spiral around plant stem

Monotreme milk

Monotremes have a unique way of breeding. They lay eggs, but they raise their young in a pouch. The young feed on their mother's milk, not from teats as in other mammals, but from glands tucked away in a groove in her pouch. These strange animals include the platypus and several kinds of echidna. They live only in New Guinea and Australia.

Adult echidna, or spiny anteater

Hairy skin lining mother's pouch

Folds of pouch held back to show egg

Recently hatched puggle inside pouch

Puggle laps up milk inside groove

Milk gland

Echidna egg
The egg is about the size of a grape, with a large yolk and a leathery shell. The female incubates it in her pouch for 10–11 days.

Hatchling puggle
The young echidna, or puggle, tears open the shell using a sharp point on its snout. At this early age, it is completely blind and has no spines.

Lapping up milk
The puggle stays in the pouch for about 55 days. The puggle has no teat to latch onto, so it laps up the mother's milk as it oozes out into a groove.

Baby boom

Instead of raising their own young, some animals trick others into doing all the work for them. The common cuckoo does this by laying eggs in the nests of smaller birds. The young cuckoo hatches first, and pushes all the other eggs or hatchlings out of the nest. From then on, it gets all the food for itself.

Foster parent feeds cuckoo, not realizing that it is an impostor

Rapidly growing cuckoo is too big to fit into nest

Mighty mouth

Peering out of a rocky crevice, one of the sea's most peculiar parents shows off a mouthful of eggs. He is a jawfish, and he collects the eggs when the female spawns. For more than a week, he protects the eggs and pumps water over them to supply them with oxygen, keeping them healthy. He releases them when they are ready to hatch.

Dark eyes of developing fish already visible within eggs

Gentle giants

In the forest of Rwanda's Volcanoes National Park, a young mountain gorilla lies in the safety of its mother's arms. Of all the great apes, mountain gorillas are the largest, but they are among the world's rarest mammals, with fewer than 800 individuals surviving in the wild. Mountain gorillas have a slow breeding rate—females give birth to a single baby every three to four years. Gorillas grow up slowly as well. This youngster will stay close to its mother until her next baby arrives, learning vital life skills such as which plants to eat, or how to build a nest in the trees for sleeping.

Instinct and learning

When turtles hatch, they scuttle straight toward the sea. Newly hatched birds beg for food from their parents, even though they cannot see. Both are examples of animal instinct—a kind of behavior that is inherited and that does not have to be learned. Instinct can make simple creatures behave in amazingly complex ways but, in most animals, instinct works hand in hand with learning. Knowledge and experience make animals better at the things they do and equip them with the skills needed for survival. Learning lets some animals develop remarkable new abilities, including making and using tools.

Headlong rush

After digging their way out of their nest in the sand, young loggerhead turtles move quickly to avoid being caught by predators. The hatchlings usually emerge on the beach after dark. Their instincts guide them toward the lightest part of the horizon and the sea. Unfortunately, many turtles are easily lured off course by the lights of beachside hotels and bars.

Feeding trigger

American robins are helpless when they hatch. Instinct makes the chicks stay still and quiet while their parents are away from the nest. The moment a parent returns with a worm, however, the young open their beaks wide and noisily beg for food. The parent bird's feeding instincts are then triggered in turn. It places the worm into the nearest open beak, guided by the brightly colored lining of the nestling's mouth and throat.

Smart cookies

Chimpanzees are our closest living relatives. They have high intelligence and use it to make different tools. Here, one chimp has made a digging stick and is using it to remove termites from a hole in their nest. The other chimp is watching closely—a sign that it will copy the technique itself when it wants to find food. As humans, we take this kind of learning for granted, but such behavior is much rarer in the animal world.

Instinct at work

Instinctive behavior is often made up of short, simple routines. Added together, they enable animals to perform astonishing feats. However, unlike learned behavior, instinctive routines are mostly fixed. For example, a potter wasp always builds the same kind of potlike nest. It does not plan ahead while it is working, and it never invents a new method.

Moving on
Common cuckoos migrate long distances each year between Europe and Africa, guided by instinct. Even on their first journey, they travel alone.

Hiding away
Young roe deer spend their first few weeks hidden from predators in long grass. Instinct makes them keep completely still, even if danger threatens.

Feeding young
Female potter wasps lay their eggs in clay nurseries. They stock each pot with caterpillars to feed the grub when it hatches. Then, they seal up the door.

Learning and play

For many young mammals, play fighting is a way of practicing important survival skills and developing the physical fitness needed for hunting. These two-month-old fox cubs are full of energy and spend much of their time playing roughly together near their den. During these fights, the cubs learn how to assert themselves in their social group, with the winner becoming the dominant cub. The cubs also follow their parents on the hunt, learning how to steer clear of danger and how to make a successful kill.

Fox cub bites and wrestles in bout of play fighting

Tools of the trade

This Egyptian vulture has picked up a stone and is about to crack open an ostrich egg. This bird's habit of using stones to get at food is based on instinct. Many other birds are tool users and some are surprisingly inventive. New Caledonian crows pick up sticks in their beaks and use these tools to tweak insects out of logs. Some have even been seen making hooks from pieces of wire—behavior that shows these birds are capable of planning ahead.

161

Living together

Some animals spend most of their lives on their own and only get together to mate. Many species, however, are social animals that reap the benefits of gathering together in large flocks, herds, or shoals. Life in a group is usually safer, and it can help animals to find more food. A few species live in highly organized societies called colonies, where members depend on each other to survive. Most of these animals are social insects, such as ants, wasps, and bees, which form giant family groups. These are often ruled by a single breeding female—the queen.

Penguin parade

Huddled together on a rocky beach, groups of adult king penguins form a stark contrast with their fluffy brown chicks. During the breeding season, as many as 100,000 adult pairs gather in huge colonies on the islands off the coast of Antarctica. These crowded breeding sites are sheltered from the snow and ice and some have been used by penguins for centuries.

Social insects

Termites live in enormous colonies of up to 25 million members—the offspring of a single queen and a breeding male, or king. In a termite nest, individual insects work together to feed and protect the colony. The termites are divided into different ranks called castes, which perform different roles within the group.

Swarm clusters around queen bee

Matriarch leads herd to water

Giving birth
With its huge sausage-shaped abdomen, a queen termite lays several thousand eggs a day. Workers feed the queen and carry her eggs to the nursery.

Caring for the young
Once the eggs have hatched, workers rear the young termites, or nymphs, in dedicated nursery areas constructed deep inside the termite nest.

Fungus farming
Some workers build underground compost heaps from their own droppings. They farm the fungus that grows on the compost and use it as food for the colony.

Defending the colony
Soldier termites protect the nest. Some are armed with powerful jaws that bite, while others squirt toxic liquids or release a gluelike substance against enemies.

Flying the nest

When a beehive gets overcrowded, the queen bee leaves, taking a large group of workers with her. Here, a swarm of honeybees has settled on a branch, while scout bees inspect possible new nesting sites for the colony. When a scout returns after finding a good site, it dances on the surface of the swarm, encouraging others to investigate its find. Once the majority of scouts agree on a new location, the entire swarm moves to its new home.

Queen for life

Naked mole rats are highly unusual mammals, because they live in large colonies, like social insects, controlled by a single breeding female known as the queen. The queen is the biggest member of each colony. She mates with up to three males and produces all of the colony's young. Some of her young take on the role of soldiers, but most become workers. The workers use their large teeth to excavate the colony's underground network of tunnels and to gnaw out food from exposed roots and tubers.

8–10 young in each litter

Up to 3 breeding males mate with queen

5–10 soldiers act as sentries and defend colony

Single queen produces and suckles young

50–200 workers dig tunnels, find food, and tend to queen and young

Safety in numbers

Swirling over a coral reef, a large shoal of smallmouth grunts make a confusing target for most predators. The fish form a tightly packed shoal and dart together in different directions to protect themselves against attack. Shoaling fish are often the same size, age, and coloring, which reduces their chances of standing out from the crowd.

Group memories

Elephants are legendary for having long memories—an ability that is crucial to the survival of family groups. This herd of female African elephants and their young is dominated by a large female called the matriarch, who may be more than 40 years old. She is responsible for the well-being of the entire family. She leads the herd to the best feeding grounds and remembers where to find water in times of drought. When the matriarch dies, the next-oldest female in the group takes her place.

The animal world

Animal evolution

The first animals were microscopic and had very simple bodies. Over millions of years, their descendants evolved into new species, with new shapes and ways of life. Evolution has produced an astonishing variety of animals, from tiny insects to colossal dinosaurs. Many species have become extinct, but others are very much alive.

Grasping, or prehensile, tail anchors body while animal attacks prey

Traces of the past

Scientists study extinct animals by looking at fossils. These show what prehistoric animals looked like and even how they behaved. Fossils form when buried remains slowly turn to stone.

Fossil bodies

Hard-bodied animals make good fossils. This fossil belongs to an extinct trilobite, which was buried by sediment on the seabed.

Trace fossils

Some fossils preserve marks that animals have left behind. This three-toed footprint was left by a carnivorous dinosaur, or theropod.

Fossil skeletons

Bone often fossilizes, although complete fossil skeletons are a lucky find. This one belongs to a crested dinosaur called *Parasaurolophus*.

Frozen bodies

Entire animals are sometimes preserved in permanently frozen ground. This baby mammoth was found in Siberia.

Stuck in amber

This insect was trapped by sticky resin oozing from a tree. The resin slowly turned to fossil amber with the insect still inside.

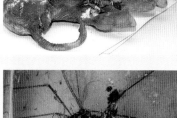

Grasping feet are an adaptation for tree-climbing lifestyle

Evolution in action

By studying living animals and fossils, scientists attempt to chart the path that evolution has followed. This family tree, or cladogram, shows how primates have evolved. The black points on the baseline mark new adaptations that have built up by evolution over millions of years. These adaptations are shared by all the animals farther along the tree.

Tarsiers

Animal species

Scientists have identified about two million kinds, or species, of animal. They are classified into about 30 major groups, called phyla. Toucans belong to the chordate phylum—a group containing all animals that have skeletons made of bone. All toucans have a similar body shape and huge bills. They look similar because they have evolved from the same distant ancestor. However, each species has its own color pattern and usually breeds only with its own kind. If toucan species interbred, their differences would blend away.

The toco toucan is the largest toucan. Unlike other toucans, it prefers open habitats with scattered trees.

The white-throated toucan is the second-largest species. It is widespread in South America's rain forests.

The channel-billed toucan differs only in slight details from the white-throated toucan. It also lives in the rain forests of South America.

The choco toucan lives in forests in western South America, where it is cut off from most other toucans by the high Andes mountains.

Animal adaptations

Leaning forward from a branch, a panther chameleon grabs a cricket with its telescopic tongue. Chameleons are lizards, but unlike most lizards, they have many features well-suited to their life in trees. Features like these are called adaptations. They develop through evolution and can affect how animals look, their behavior, and the way their bodies work. Some adaptations have proved to be a runaway success. These breakthroughs include skeletons made of bone, which first evolved more than 450 million years ago, and insect wings, which date back nearly as far. They have helped to make vertebrates and insects two of the most successful animal groups on Earth.

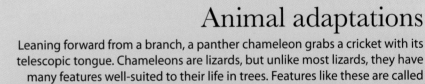

Long, sucker-tipped tongue can catch food on neighboring twigs

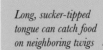

Cricket is too slow to evade tongue attack

New World monkeys

Old World monkeys

Gibbons

Great apes and humans

- Mobile face with lips that can protrude
- Single pair of nipples on chest

- Two premolar teeth
- Nostrils close together
- All fingers and toes with nails, not claws

- Highly mobile shoulder joints
- Can move for limited periods when standing on hind legs

- Skeleton suited to upright or semi-upright stance
- Highly enlarged brain

Sponges

Living mainly in the sea, sponges are simple animals with skeletons made of mineral crystals and protein fibers. They live by pumping water through a system of holes, or pores, and filtering out particles of food. The largest kinds are more than 6½ ft (2 m) tall and can be more than 100 years old.

In tubular sponges, water flows in through pores in the sides and out through a vent at the top.

Invertebrates

Invertebrates make up the vast majority of animals. They have an extraordinary variety of shapes, although none has a backbone or any kind of bony skeleton. The total number of species is unknown, but may be more than 10 million.

Flatworms

Flatworms have thin, flat bodies without blood or a heart. Most live in water or in damp habitats on land, but some kinds are parasites living inside other animals.

Turbellarians are free-living predators or scavengers up to 2 ft (60 cm) long. On land, they move by creeping.

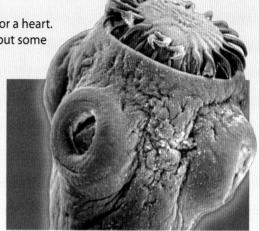

A parasitic tapeworm attaches its ribbonlike body to the intestines of vertebrates with suckers and hooks on its head.

Jellyfish, sea anemones, and corals

These invertebrates all have simple bodies with a ring of stinging tentacles around a central mouth. Jellyfish and sea anemones are usually predatory. Reef-building corals often contain microscopic algae, which provide them with some of their food.

Jellyfish have a bell-shaped body trailing stinging tentacles. Some species contain algae and often rest upside down.

Sea anemones live on the seabed. They are often brightly colored with long, stinging tentacles and a suckerlike base.

Soft corals have fleshy or leathery bodies forming colonies with spreading, plantlike shapes.

Reef-building corals live in colonies that build hard, chalky skeletons. The tiny animals occupy cups within the skeleton.

Roundworms

Compared to other worms, roundworms all look similar. They are round in cross-section and do not have segments. They have a tough outer skin, or cuticle, and a tapering head and tail. Roundworms are extremely common in wet and damp habitats and as parasites of animals and plants.

A parasitic roundworm's body moves by curling and uncurling.

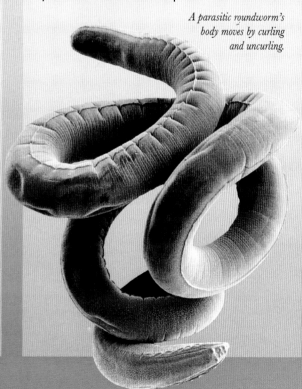

Segmented worms

Worms in the "segmented worms" group have many different shapes, but their bodies are always divided into repeated units, or segments. Some burrow, while others crawl or swim. Some are parasitic.

These giant tube worms live only around deep-sea volcanic vents and grow up to 7¾ ft (2.4 m) long.

Earthworms move through soil and leaf litter by expanding and contracting their segments in a sequence.

Predatory ragworms can crawl and swim with their leglike flaps. Their heads bristle with feelers.

Fan worms live in tubes and filter food from water using a retractable crown of tentacles.

Sea mice are covered with iridescent "fur." They burrow through the seabed in search of prey.

Echinoderms

Starfish and their relatives are called echinoderms, which means "spiny skin." They are sea creatures covered with spines or knobs and are usually made of five equal parts. They move by snaking their arms or by creeping on their spines and tiny fluid-filled feet.

Beneath a starfish's stiff arms are hundreds of tube feet. Starfish eat slow-moving or fixed animals, such as corals and clams.

Brittle stars have long, highly flexible arms, which they use to scavenge dead animals and waste on the seabed.

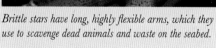

Living on the seabed, sea cucumbers have a cluster of tentacles around the mouth that collect food.

Sea urchins are algae-eating inhabitants of rocky shores and reefs. They are encased by a chalky covering with many spines.

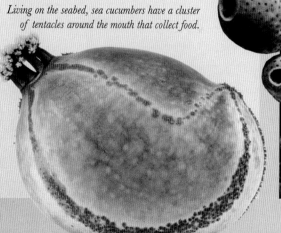

Sea squirts

Adult sea squirts have bag-shaped bodies and live by filtering particles of food. Their young look like tadpoles, with a body stiffened by a rod, or notochord—a sign that they are closely related to vertebrates.

Sea squirts have a leathery body with openings for sucking in water and pumping it out. They often live in groups.

Mollusks

With more than 90,000 species, few invertebrate groups are more varied than mollusks. Their most noticeable feature is often their shell. Not all mollusks have one, but for most, it provides protection from attack. Mollusks typically move by creeping, but this group also includes fast swimmers, such as octopuses and squid.

Chitons

A chiton's shell is made of eight hinged plates surrounded by a muscular girdle. Underneath is a suckerlike foot, which chitons use to clamp themselves to rocks. Chitons live in the sea and feed mainly on algae. Like snails, they scrape up their food with a ribbonlike tongue, or radula, armed with hundreds of microscopic, toothlike denticles.

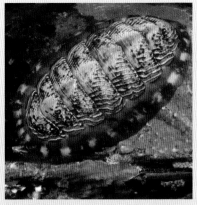

This chiton is attached to a rock in a tidal pool. Its head is pointing to the left.

Gastropods

Snails and their relatives make up a group called the gastropods. Most have a coiled shell, produced by a body layer called the mantle, and a suckerlike foot. Gastropods are very common in the sea, but many species live on land.

Land snails' eyes are on a long pair of retractable tentacles. They breath air through a space in their mantle that acts like a lung.

Abalones graze algae on rocky shores. Their shells are iridescent on the inside, and people make jewelry from them.

Land slugs look like land snails without a shell, but some have a tiny internal shell called a shell plate.

To drift across oceans, bubble raft snails use a raft made from bubbles of mucus. Their shells are wafer-thin.

Conches are large tropical sea snails with thick, heavy shells. They move by flicking a hard-edged foot.

Limpets graze on algae and live on rocks exposed to waves. They have strong suckers and simple conical shells.

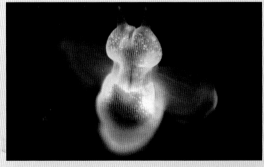

Cowries can extend their mantle up and over their egg-shaped, glossy shell. Both shell and mantle may be brightly patterned.

Sea slugs don't have shells. These creeping marine gastropods are often vividly colored, with external gills and horns.

Sea butterflies are sea snails that live in open water. Their foot extends sideways and beats like a pair of wings.

Bivalves

A bivalve's shell has two parts joined by a hinge. If danger strikes, most bivalves close their shells, sealing themselves inside. Bivalves always live in water, except seashore ones exposed at low tide. Also known as clams, most of them are filter-feeders, although giant clams get some of their food from microscopic algae, which live in their multicolored lips.

The giant clams of coral reefs can grow up to 4 ft (1.2 m) across.

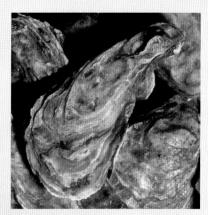

Cockles are saltwater clams that burrow into sediment on muddy shores, using a muscular foot.

Scallops clap their shells together to swim. They have two rows of eyes along the shell opening.

Razor clams have long, slender, rectangular shells and can dig rapidly into sand and mud.

Mussels attach themselves permanently to rocks with tough elastic threads.

Oysters live in estuaries and lagoons, where they stay permanently in oyster beds on the mud.

Cephalopods

Fast-moving and intelligent predators, cephalopods have arms with suckers and can swim by squirting a jet of water, although squid and cuttlefish also ripple their fins. Nautiluses have spiral shells, but other cephalopods have an internal shell, or no shell at all. They live in the sea, sometimes at great depths.

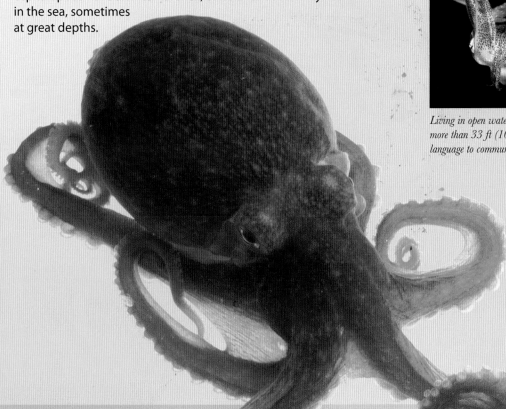

Living in open water, squid include giant species more than 33 ft (10 m) long. Some use body language to communicate threat.

Cuttlefish are experts at color change. They shoot out two long tentacles to catch their prey.

Octopuses' bulbous heads contain large brains and beaklike jaws. Their eight arms are connected by webs of skin. Some use these webs to sail on currents near the seabed.

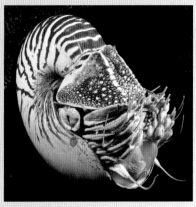

Nautiluses have up to 90 short tentacles and a shell with gas-filled chambers that keep it afloat.

171

Arthropods

All arthropods have jointed legs and an external case, or exoskeleton. They form an enormous group of invertebrates, dominated by insects, but also including a huge variety of other animals on land and in water.

Horseshoe crabs

Despite their name, horseshoe crabs are more closely related to spiders than to crabs. These armored arthropods have five pairs of walking legs hidden by a shield, or carapace. They eat animals, using pincers to pluck them from the seabed. There are just four living species.

A horseshoe crab has a hinge between its rounded carapace and its abdomen.

Crustaceans

Ranging from bulky lobsters to tiny water fleas, crustaceans live mainly in water. Their exoskeleton is often reinforced with calcium, forming a hard crust.

Lobsters use powerful claws to crack open mollusks on the seabed.

Crabs scavenge the shore and seabed with their two pincers. Their tails are tucked underneath their broad shells, or carapaces.

Krill form immense swarms in the open ocean. These shrimplike filter-feeders are a key food for baleen whales.

Barnacles spend their adult lives stuck to rocks or floating objects. They filter-feed with limbs protruding from their hard cases.

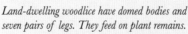
Land-dwelling woodlice have domed bodies and seven pairs of legs. They feed on plant remains.

Water fleas swim by flicking branched antennae. They are tiny filter-feeders that are very common in freshwater.

Arachnids

Living mainly on land, arachnids usually have four pairs of legs. Most are carnivorous, and many have venomous bites or stings. Spiders make up the largest single group of arachnids, followed by mites and ticks.

Ground-dwelling predators, scorpions are armed with pincers and venomous stings.

Unlike true spiders, sun-spiders lack poison, so they use powerful pincers to kill and chew up their prey.

Orb-web spiders weave flat, spiral webs. Some species have spines and vivid warning colors.

Tarantulas are giant spiders that hunt on the ground or in trees, finding prey mainly by touch.

Sea spiders

Sea spiders are not closely related to spiders that live on land, even though they usually have eight legs. Their heads are tiny and their bodies extremely slender, with long legs that end in hooks. They are most common in shallow water, although some live on the deep seabed.

Sea spiders clamber over seaweeds, rocks, and corals, feeding on animals and dead remains.

Springtails

Closely related to insects, springtails have six legs but no wings. If disturbed, they flick their tubular tails, which catapults them through the air. Most springtails are tiny. They are extremely common in leaf litter, on plants, and on the surface of pools and ponds.

Some species of springtails feed on the surface of plants. Some cause serious damage to crops.

Small and sharp-eyed, jumping spiders hunt by day, leaping through the air onto their prey.

Centipedes

A centipede's body is made of many segments, each with a single pair of legs. Centipedes are carnivorous. Their flat bodies let them squeeze through crevices in search of prey.

A typical centipede has a poisonous claw, used to kill its prey, on each side of its head.

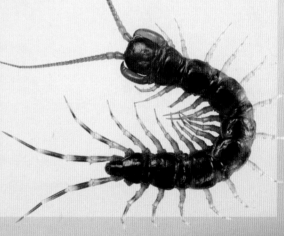

House centipedes' long, slender legs propel them at great speed. They are common indoors in many parts of the world.

Mites include house dust mites, which are microscopic scavengers that feed on flakes of skin in household dust.

Millipedes

Unlike centipedes, millipedes have cylindrical bodies with two pairs of legs on each segment. The total number of legs varies from fewer than 50 to more than 700. They feed on the decaying remains of plants.

A millipede's exoskeleton is reinforced with hard minerals, but it may also defend itself by coiling up and producing vile toxic chemicals.

Ticks are bloodsucking parasites. This mating pair shows a small male on top of a female swollen with a meal of blood.

Insects

With more than 800,000 species identified so far, insects make up the biggest group of arthropods. Adult insects have six legs and most have two pairs of wings. When insects grow up, they change in shape, undergoing partial or complete metamorphosis.

Dragonflies

Adult dragonflies catch insects in midair. Some patrol in search of food, while others dart from a perch. Dragonflies spend the first part of their lives in freshwater, as predatory nymphs. These have hinged mouthparts that can shoot forward, grabbing their prey.

Dragonflies' transparent wings stay spread at rest, not folded like those of most other insects.

Partial transformers

Insects in this group undergo a slight change in shape, or partial metamorphosis. Their young, known as nymphs, look similar to their parents, although they have small wing buds instead of working wings. Each time they molt, their wing buds get larger. After the final molt, the nymph becomes an adult. Nymphs and adults often live in the same surroundings and eat the same kinds of food.

Grasshoppers typically have tough, leathery forewings. Their hind wings are large, but they usually escape predators by jumping with powerful hind legs.

Katydids have threadlike antennae that are often longer than their bodies.

Earwigs' abdomens are tipped by curved pincers. Their hind wings fold beneath stubby forewings.

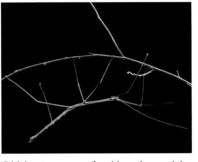

Stick insects are camouflaged in undergrowth by their extraordinary twiglike bodies.

Cockroaches sense vibration and flee fast from danger, squeezing their flat bodies into crevices.

Termites often form huge colonies that build elaborate nests. Some chew on wood, which they digest with the help of microorganisms in the gut. Others are important grazers in grasslands.

Praying mantises hunt insects, catching them with a swift strike of their barbed forelegs.

Like many true bugs, cicadas drink plant sap with piercing mouthparts. Adult males sing loudly.

Thorn bugs, or treehoppers, suck sap secretly, disguised as one of the plant's thorns.

Water bugs grip prey with their forelegs while sucking it dry with their syringelike mouths.

Complete transformers

Instead of changing slowly, insects in this group undergo an abrupt change in shape, or complete metamorphosis. Their young, or larvae, usually look nothing like their parents, with no sign of wings and sometimes no legs. Many are called grubs or maggots. The larvae usually live in a different habitat from their parents and eat a different kind of food. When a larva is mature, it enters a resting stage called a pupa or chrysalis. Its body is dismantled, and an adult's body built in its place.

Goliath beetles are Earth's heaviest insects, weighing up to 3 ½ oz (100 g).

Ladybugs are brightly colored beetles that feed on aphids and other sap-sucking insects.

There are nearly 50,000 types of weevil, each with dainty jaws at the end of a long snout.

Often bright or metallic, leaf beetles eat plants, including crops such as potatoes.

Fierce diving beetles swim in freshwater using their hind legs. The larvae are called water tigers.

Mosquitoes suck blood with their syringelike mouths. Like all flies, they have only two wings.

Houseflies liquefy their food by spitting onto it. They then suck it up with spongelike mouthparts.

Horseflies drink with their lapping mouthparts. They are blood-feeders that slice into their prey.

Fleas suck blood while living aboard mammals and birds. They are wingless, but good jumpers.

All wasps have stings, but some live in delicate group nests, which they build from chewed wood.

Bumblebees are large bees with furlike scales. They feed on pollen and nectar from flowers.

Some members of honey ant nests have swollen abdomens that store liquid food.

Morpho butterflies have large, iridescent wings. Their forelegs are tiny and brush-shaped.

Hawk moths are large, powerful flyers with narrow wings. Most feed at flowers.

Swallowtails, like most butterflies, drink nectar with their long, curved tongues. Their caterpillars deter predators with a foul-smelling, forked scent organ, or osmeterium.

Atlas moths have the largest wingspans of all insects, measuring up to 11 in (28 cm).

Fish

Fish live, breathe, and swim in fresh or saltwater. They have inner skeletons, including skull, ribs, and backbone. Fish extract oxygen from the water using gills and swim using their tail and fins. A fish's skin is covered in tough scales.

Bony fish

Most species of fish are members of the bony fish group. They have a skeleton of bone and most are covered in overlapping scales. Bony fish come in all shapes and sizes and survive in almost every water habitat. There are more than 25,000 species alive today.

Jawless fish

Hagfish and lampreys are long, slimy, eel-like fish with no biting jaws. Hagfish are not true fish, or even true vertebrates, since they lack a backbone. They do have a skull, though, and are the closest living relatives of true fish.

Lampreys attach their round sucker mouths to aquatic animals and bite through the flesh to suck the blood.

Hagfish have four hearts and a slitlike mouth surrounded by tentacles. If threatened, they release a sticky slime.

Catfish have prominent touch organs, or barbels, that resemble a cat's whiskers. They use them to search for food.

Like all bottom-dwelling flatfish, the yellowtail flounder has eyes that are both located on one side of the head.

Cartilaginous fishes

Sharks, rays, and deep-water chimaeras have an internal skeleton made of flexible cartilage rather than bone. Special sense organs allow cartilaginous fish to track other animals by detecting their electrical fields.

Hammerhead sharks are named after their unusually shaped heads. Eyes and nostrils are located on each end.

The manta ray is the largest of the rays. It can measure 25 ft (7.5 m) across and lives in tropical seas.

Clownfish live within the stinging tentacles of sea anemones, which are poisonous to other fish.

The gray reef shark swims in waters around coral reefs. It feeds on bony fish and crustaceans.

The fins on a common skate fan out from its head, giving it its distinctive shape.

The Atlantic sailfish uses its long bill to stun and kill its prey.

176

Coelacanths were thought to have died out with the dinosaurs, but were rediscovered in 1938.

Lungfish can survive for months in dry conditions when sealed up in mud cocoons.

The skeleton of the stellate sturgeon is part bone, part cartilage. People eat its eggs as caviar.

The eyes of deep-ocean-dwelling hatchetfish point upward to spot prey overhead.

The blue ribbon eel buries itself in sand or hides behind rocks, dashing out to feed on small fish.

Sea horses mate for life. The male carries eggs in his brood pouch until they hatch.

The blind cave fish has no eyes, but it is able to navigate the dark waters in deep Mexican caves.

Atlantic herring swim in huge shoals, often numbering hundreds of thousands.

The fanfin anglerfish uses a bulbous stalk over its head as bait to lure prey.

Sockeye salmon swim from ocean to river to lay eggs, or spawn.

The rosy-lipped batfish uses its fins like legs to crawl around the ocean floor.

The tailbar lion fish uses its long, poisonous spines for defense.

Porcupinefish warn off potential predators by inflating their bodies with water.

The colorful moorish idol uses its long snout to reach morsels of food in crevices in coral reefs.

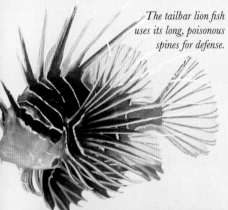

The leafy sea dragon has leaflike protrusions all over its body, disguising it as seaweed.

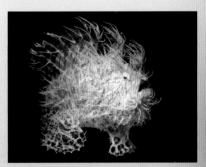

Hairy frogfish sit on the ocean floor waiting to suck passing prey into their cavernous mouths.

Amphibians

Earth's 5,000 kinds of amphibian are thin-skinned animals and need to stay moist. Most of them breed by laying eggs in freshwater. They usually start life as swimming tadpoles, or larvae, which slowly change shape and move onto land.

Frogs and toads

Unlike other amphibians, adult frogs and toads do not have tails. Their hind legs are often larger than the front pair, and they can have webbed feet or separate toes. Experts are not in agreement on which of these animals are called frogs and which are toads. Most frogs and toads breed in water, although some lay their eggs in trees, leaving their tadpoles to drop into pools and streams.

Caecilians

These wormlike amphibians live only in the tropics (near the equator). They have no legs and many spend all their lives in the soil.

Typical caecilians have a cylindrical body divided into rings, with a wedge-shaped snout used for burrowing.

A male crested newt's conspicuous crest develops only when adults return to water to breed.

Amazonian horned frogs have thickset, camouflaged bodies, large mouths, and a prominent horn above each eye.

Poison dart frogs are small, highly toxic rain forest amphibians that often have conspicuous warning colors.

Salamanders and newts

Most of the animals in this group are called salamanders. Some live on land, but most breed in water. Newts are members of just one family.

The Eastern newt starts life in water as a tadpolelike larva. It then spends 1–4 years as a bright-red juvenile, before transforming again into an aquatic adult.

Mole salamander larvae have feathery gills and some can breed without transforming into land-dwelling adults.

Flying frogs live in rain forests. Their large, webbed feet allow them to parachute from tree to tree.

The fire salamander's colors warn predators that it is toxic.

Lungless salamanders breathe through their skin and the lining of their mouths. Many live entirely on land.

Rain frogs shelter underground during the dry season, coming to the surface after rain to eat insects.

Tongueless frogs spend their lives in water. They lack a tongue and some have a flat, leaflike body.

Asian horned frogs live on rain forest floors and mimic fallen leaves.

Spadefoot toads burrow with their back legs, spending dry periods underground.

The crucifix toad has cross-shaped markings and is suited to burrowing in dry habitats.

True toads, such as this cane toad, have warty skin and a bulging poison gland behind each eye.

The red-eyed tree frog has sticky toe-pads and startling forward-facing eyes.

Typical adult tree frogs may never return to water. They often lay their eggs above ground.

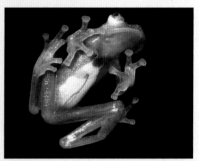

Glass frogs have translucent skin on their bellies. They lay their eggs on leaves overhanging water.

The goliath frog is the world's largest frog. Its body can grow to a length of 14 in (35 cm).

North American bullfrog males have an inflatable throat pouch and a deep, powerful call.

Leopard frogs have powerful back legs, and the male has two inflatable vocal sacs.

Mantellas are small, brightly colored frogs with toxic skin. They live only in Madagascar.

File-eared tree frogs have jagged ridges above the ears. They lay eggs in foam nests on branches.

The Mexican burrowing frog lives mainly underground, emerging only after heavy rain.

The tomato frog is a type of narrow-mouthed frog. Its bright color warns that its skin produces a sticky, toxic substance when threatened.

A male Darwin's frog carries his tadpoles in his vocal sac until they emerge as froglets.

Narrow-mouthed frogs usually specialize in eating ants and termites.

Reptiles

With their scaly skin, reptiles thrive in places with hot, dry climates, although they live in many other habitats as well. There are about 8,000 species. Most of them breed by laying eggs, but some produce live young.

Lizards and snakes

By far the most common reptiles, lizards and snakes are close relatives and form a single group. Snakes are always carnivorous, and most lizards are as well, although some kinds eat plants or animal remains. The majority lay eggs, but in cold regions, many give birth to live young.

Iguanas are plant-eating, tree-dwelling lizards. Their long claws help them to climb, and the males of some species attract females by displaying a fleshy dewlap hanging from their necks.

Tuataras

Living only in New Zealand, tuataras belong to an ancient group of reptiles. Instead of true teeth, they have a jagged edge to their jaw.

Both sexes of tuatara have a spiny crest. They grow very slowly and may live for more than 100 years.

Turtles and tortoises

Recognizable by their shells, or carapaces, most animals in this group are turtles. The tortoises form a single land-based family.

The Indian starred tortoise's shell becomes increasingly knobby with age and has distinctive starlike markings.

Chameleons are slow-moving tree-dwellers with grasping feet and swiveling eyes. They are capable of rapid color change.

With a shell up to 4 ft (1.2 m) long, these Galápagos giant tortoises are among the largest animals in the tortoise family.

The matamata is a camouflaged river turtle that ambushes prey, sucking fish into its mouth.

The Gila monster's colorful patterning warns predators that it is one of very few venomous lizards.

Like other sea turtles, the green turtle is streamlined, with winglike front flippers.

The enormous leatherback turtle has a rubbery carapace up to 6 ft (1.8 m) long and can weigh nearly a ton.

Venomous coral snakes show bright warning colors. Some nonvenomous snakes mimic their pattern.

Geckos do not have eyelids, so they lick their eyes clean instead of blinking.

Male anoles extend their colored throat fans to signal to rival males and potential mates.

Basilisks live near water and escape danger by running across the surface.

Crocodilians

The world's biggest reptiles belong to this group of heavily armored predators. Expert swimmers and divers, they often lurk in the shallows, where they attack animals at the water's edge. They breed by laying eggs. Unusually for reptiles, they look after their young.

Protective spines cover the thorny devil's bizarre body. It eats ants in the Australian desert.

The male rainbow agama's vivid courtship colors contrast with camouflaged females.

The Australian frilled lizard has a peculiar neck frill used to startle potential predators.

Caimans bury themselves in mud during droughts. They live in Central and South American rivers.

Skinks have short legs and smooth, shiny scales. Some reveal bright blue tongues if threatened.

Wall lizards often blend in with rocks and plants. They are agile, fast-moving insect-eaters.

The slowworm is a legless lizard with a snakelike body. It gives birth to live young.

Compared to crocodiles, alligators have a broad, rounded snout. They live for around 50 years.

The largest monitor lizards grow to a length of 10 ft (3 m) and pack a venomous bite.

Boas and pythons lack venom, but they kill by squeezing with their heavy, muscular bodies.

Green and extremely slender, vine snakes are well hidden up in the trees, where they live.

The largest crocodiles are the biggest living reptiles, with a length of up to 20 ft (6 m).

Cobras open their hooded necks during threat displays. They are highly venomous.

Sea kraits are venomous fish-eaters with tails like paddles. They return to land to lay eggs.

Vipers' long, hinged fangs swing forward and deliver venom when attacking prey.

Gharials' extremely slender snouts move quickly though the water to snap up fish.

Birds

Unlike reptiles, birds are warm-blooded. They have wings and feathers, although not all of them can fly. Most birds take care of their young until they are ready to leave the nest. There are about 10,000 species of bird.

Ratites

With weak wing muscles and flat breast bones, ratites cannot fly. They escape danger by running away.

Kiwis are the smallest ratites. Their plumage is hairlike, their bills are long, and their sense of smell is very strong.

The ostrich is Earth's largest bird and the fastest runner. It stands up to 9 ft (2.7 m) tall.

New birds

All birds other than ratites, waterfowl, and fowl belong to a huge group that scientists call Neoaves, or "new birds," because they appear recently in the fossil record. All of these birds have powerful wing muscles and most are completely at home in the air. The largest flyers include albatrosses, storks, and pelicans, but the most varied are small songbirds, or passerines. These make up about one-third of all bird species.

Albatrosses soar on outstretched, narrow wings. One tracked bird traveled 3,700 miles (6,000 km) in 12 days.

Gulls live in large, noisy groups along coasts and inland waterways and some scavenge on human garbage.

Fowl and waterfowl

Fowl are chickenlike birds with strong legs and feet. They fly well over short distances, although they spend most of their lives on the ground. Waterfowl usually have webbed feet. They are good swimmers and feed in water or on land.

Male ducks, such as this mandarin, are often brightly colored, which helps them to attract a mate.

A swan can fly at more than 30 mph (50 kph), but to get its heavy body airborne involves running and flapping.

All hummingbirds weigh less than 1 oz (24 g) and some beat their wings up to 200 times a second during courtship.

The male peafowl, or peacock, will erect his fan of extravagant tail feathers to attract peahens during courtship.

Male grouse have showy courtship rituals. In this dance, the females prefer the males that rest the least.

Birds of paradise live in tropical forests. Males have spectacular plumage and elaborate courtship displays.

Penguins cannot fly but they swim gracefully. On ice they waddle or slide on their stomachs.

Grebes eat fish and have paddle-shaped toes. They often carry their young on their backs.

Flamingos have long legs and necks and bent beaks that they use upside down to filter food.

Waders, such as this avocet, feed on shorelines and in wetlands. Most have long legs and many have long bills, which they use to probe into mud for worms and clams.

With long legs, herons hunt by stealth in the shallows, using their beaks to stab their prey.

Some pelicans fish by dive-bombing, scooping up fish with their pouched beaks.

Bald eagles have a hind talon on each foot that pierces fish as the bird grabs them from the water.

Auks, which include puffins, live on the coast and dive for fish, using their wings to swim.

Pigeons have plump bodies and eat seeds and fruit. Some have large crests.

Macaws have long tails and colorful plumage. They are the largest flying parrots.

As nocturnal hunters, owls hide by day, camouflaged by their mottled plumage.

Swifts hardly ever land, except when nesting. They eat insects and even sleep in midair.

Woodpeckers have chisel-like beaks. They hammer holes in trees to reach insect grubs.

Toucans live in the tropics and eat fruit with enormous and often brightly colored beaks.

Kingfishers return to a favorite perch after a catch, striking the fish before swallowing it.

Icterids use their sharply pointed beaks to force open gaps to get at hidden food.

Wood warblers eat insects with their short, pointed beaks and typically nest in woodlands.

The largest songbirds are crows, which are often adaptable and intelligent but have harsh calls.

Monotremes

The only egg-laying mammals, monotremes include the platypus, which feeds in water, and spiny anteaters, or echidnas, which live on land. Unlike other mammals, female monotremes lack nipples. They ooze milk onto their skin, and their young lap it up.

Echidnas eat insects using their long snouts and sticky tongues. They have powerful legs with huge claws that they use for digging and tearing open logs.

Marsupials

Most marsupials raise their young inside a pouch. Nipples inside the pouch provide the young with milk. Kangaroos and koalas usually give birth to a single offspring. Opossums can give birth to several dozen, although not all survive.

American opossums will eat almost anything, including poisonous snakes. They often live in trees and are agile climbers with scaly, grasping tails and sharp claws.

Young koalas eat their mothers' feces, or pap, which gives them the bacteria they will need to digest eucalyptus leaves, their main food source.

Mammals

Mammals are hairy, warm-blooded animals that feed their young on milk. Except for monotremes, all give birth to live offspring. Marsupials are tiny when they are born, but other mammals often emerge well developed. There are about 5,400 species. They live on land and in water.

Aardvark

This African mammal has no close relatives and is classified on its own. It eats termites and ants, breaking into their nests with its powerful front claws. With keen senses of hearing and smell but poor eyesight, it hides during the day in deep burrows.

The aardvark's protruding snout contains a long, sticky tongue that can reach deep into insect nests.

Elephants

Instantly recognizable by their long trunks, elephants are the biggest land animals. They have pillarlike legs, enormous ears, and long incisor teeth, or tusks. Elephants use their tusks to break open tree trunks and to dig for water and salt.

The African savanna elephant is the largest elephant species. Some males weigh more than 7½ tons (7 metric tons).

Sea cows

Unlike seals, sea cows feed entirely on plants. These large, aquatic mammals include the dugong, which lives along shallow tropical coasts, and manatees, which also venture into rivers. All have barrel-shaped bodies and a lobed or paddle-shaped tail.

A manatees' flippers swing forward to hold plants when feeding. Its mouth has a grasping, or prehensile, upper lip.

Anteaters and relatives

Anteaters, armadillos, and sloths form a single group of related mammals. They look different, but they share telltale features, such as unusual joints in their backbones. Anteaters and armadillos eat small animals, but sloths live in trees and feed on leaves.

Tamanduas are tree-climbing anteaters with grasping tails. They have long tongues but no teeth.

Primates

Most primates have grasping hands and feet and forward-facing eyes. The group includes monkeys, apes, lemurs, bushbabies, and tarsiers.

Bushbabies, also known as galagos, have excellent night vision and hearing. They can also jump up to 6½ ft (2 m) vertically.

Living in forest treetops, marmosets use their long teeth to chew holes in tree trunks and branches to feed on the gum inside.

Chimpanzees belong to a family of primates called the great apes, which also includes gorillas, orangutans, and humans. They are intelligent, highly social apes that feed on the ground and in trees.

Rodents and rabbits

Rodents make up more than two-fifths of the world's mammal species. Like rabbits and hares, they gnaw their food with their large incisor teeth, which grow nonstop.

Squirrels use their keen sense of smell to locate nuts they buried previously. Many have bushy tails that they use for balance.

Hares and rabbits are related to rodents. To get more nutrients from their food, they digest it twice—by eating their own dung.

Many mice and rats breed at a rapid rate, producing up to 12 young every six weeks or so.

The capybara is the world's largest rodent, weighing up to 145 lb (65 kg). It escapes predators by swimming.

Pangolins

A pangolin is covered with protective, overlapping scales. Pangolins feed on ants and termites and do not have teeth.

A tree pangolin's grasping tail anchors the animal when climbing and feeding in trees.

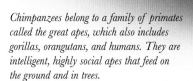
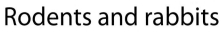

Moles, hedgehogs, and shrews

These mammals all have sharp teeth, small eyes, and a keen sense of smell. Most feed on insects and earthworms, although hedgehogs are omnivorous.

Moles have short, velvety fur and live in tunnels they dig with shovel-like front paws.

Hedgehogs forage at night. If attacked, they roll into a ball to use their spines as protection.

Bats

With wings made of skin, bats are the only flying mammals. Small kinds usually feed on insects, while large ones feed mainly at flowers and on fruit.

Fruit bats have large eyes and most roost in trees. Their wings span up to 6 ft (1.8 m).

Vampire bats have good eyesight and sharp teeth and feed on mammal and bird blood.

Carnivores

Closely related to one another, many meat-eating mammals form a group called the carnivores. These include the world's biggest land predators. Carnivores' teeth are the right shapes for gripping and slicing meat. Most are fast and agile, with forward-facing eyes, claws, and a keen sense of hearing and smell. Some carnivores eat nothing but meat, but others have mixed diets. The giant panda feeds almost entirely on one plant—bamboo.

The tiger is the largest member of the cat family. Once widespread in Asia, it is now critically endangered.

Brown bears are the largest land predators. Those that eat mainly meat grow to twice the weight of those that eat mainly plants.

Many mongooses live in burrows that were dug by other animals. They often mark their new territory, and their young, with scent.

Badgers often live in social groups in large, underground burrows, or setts, and come out at night to find food.

Many members of the dog family, such as wolves, are pack-forming predators that use speed and endurance to catch prey.

Harp seals are born on ice. Many spend their lives cruising the chilly waters of the Arctic Ocean feeding on fish and crustaceans.

Horses and relatives

Tapirs, horses, and rhinos are hoofed mammals, or ungulates, with an uneven number of toes. Tapirs and rhinos are usually solitary, but horses and their relatives live mainly in herds, relying on speed and endurance to escape danger.

Tapirs use their prehensile trunks to pluck fruit from branches.

Zebras belong to the horse family. Their stripes may encourage them to form social bonds and groom one another.

Rhino horns can grow up to 5 ft (1.5 m) long. Females use theirs to protect their young, while males use them to battle attackers.

Antelopes, deer, and relatives

Most hoofed mammals, or ungulates, belong to this group, which includes many types of wild sheep, goats, and cattle. These mammals have an even number of toes and many have long, slender legs. The majority live entirely on plant food.

The giraffe is the world's tallest animal and can reach leaves up to 16 ft (5 m) above the ground.

Male deer use their bony antlers when fighting over females. They grow new ones every year.

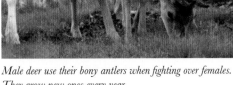

A camel can travel up to 100 miles (160 km) across the desert using the water it produces from the fat in its hump.

Gerenuks, a type of antelope, often stand up on their hind legs to reach leaves on tall bushes that other species cannot reach.

Whales

Ranging in size from porpoises to blue whales—Earth's largest animals—whales breathe through blowholes and swim with flippers and tail flukes.

Baleen whales have mouths that are full of fibrous baleen plates, which work like sieves to filter their food from the water.

Toothed whales include dolphins, porpoises, and sperm whales. Many use echolocation to find their prey.

Index

188

Acknowledgments

Dorling Kindersley would like to thank: Matilda Gollon for editing the jacket, Lili Bryant for editorial assistance, Caitlin Doyle for proofreading, and Helen Peters for the index.

Picture credits
The publisher would like to thank the following for their kind permission to reproduce their photographs:

(Key: a-above; b-below/bottom; c-center; f-far; l-left; r-right; t-top)

1 Alamy Images: Steve Bloom Images (bc). **Corbis:** John Pitcher / Design Pics (bl). **FLPA:** Chris Newbert / Minden Pictures (br). **Getty Images:** Thomas Shahan / Flickr (bl). **Photolibrary:** Alaskastock. **2–3 Ardea:** Chris Brunskill. **3 Getty Images:** Eastcott Momatiuk (bc); Visuals Unlimited (br); Max Gibbs / Photolibrary (fbl). **naturepl.com:** Charlie Hamilton-James (bl). **Splashdowndirect.com:** Andre Seale (fbr). **4 Corbis:** Stephen Frink (cla). **Andras Meszaros:** (clb). **naturepl.com:** Neil Lucas (cl). **NHPA / Photoshot:** Kevin Schafer (bl). **4–5 Getty Images:** Daisy Gilardini. **5 Corbis:** DLILLC (cla). **Getty Images:** Digital Vision (bl); Pal Hermansen (tl). **Louis-Marie Préau:** (clb). **Science Photo Library:** Byron Jorjorian (cl). **6 Corbis:** Richard Cummins (crb); George Steinmetz (fcrb). **FLPA:** Derek Middleton (cb). **Getty Images:** Stuart Westmorland (clb). **Scubazoo.com:** Jason Isley (fclb). **6–7 Corbis:** Stephen Frink. **8 Corbis:** Clouds Hill Imaging Ltd. (clb). **NHPA / Photoshot:** Burt Jones & Maurine Shimlock (bl). **8–9 Scubazoo.com:** Jason Isley. **9 Corbis:** Norbert Wu / Science Faction (tr). **FLPA:** Piotr Naskrecki / Minden Pictures (bc). **10 Getty Images:** Mike Kemp (tr); Stuart Westmorland (bl). **Science Photo Library:** David Hall (br). **10–11 Photolibrary:** Paul Kay. **11 Alamy Images:** Gregory Davies (tl). **FLPA:** Chris Newbert / Minden Pictures (br). **12–13 FLPA:** Derek Middleton. **13 Ardea:** Becca Saunders (bl). **Corbis:** Visuals Unlimited (cr) (crb); Herbert Kehrer (br). **NHPA / Photoshot:** James Carmichael Jr. (tc). **14–15 FLPA:** Chris Newbert / Minden Pictures. **16 FLPA:** Norbert Wu / Minden Pictures (cla). **17 Science Photo Library:** D. Roberts (br). **18 FLPA:** Piotr Naskrecki / Minden Pictures. **18–19 Corbis:** Ralph A. Clevenger (t). **19 Corbis:** Peter Johnson (c); David A. Northcott (cra); Paul Souders (bl). **Getty Images:** David Doubilet / National Geographic (br). **NHPA / Photoshot:** Martin Harvey (cr). **20 Getty Images:** Joseph Vans Os (cl). **Science Photo Library:** British Antarctic Survey (c). **20–21 FLPA:** John Eveson. **21 Getty Images:** Doug Allan (cla); Eastcott Momatiuk (cb). **Science Photo Library:** Power and Syred (cr); T-Service (br). **22 FLPA:** Erica Olsen (bl). **22–23 Getty Images:** Daniel Beltra. **23 naturepl.com:** Phil Savoie (clb); Dave Watts (tl). **Science Photo Library:** Power and Syred (cb). **24–25 Corbis:** Richard Cummins. **26 Corbis:** Ralph Clevenger (bl); Randy Faris (cl); George Steinmetz (tc). **Science Photo Library:** Eye of Science (cb). **27 Corbis:** Tim Davies (tr). **naturepl.com:** Edwin Giesbers (b); Andy Sands (tl). **Science Photo Library:** Eye of Science (ca). **28–29 naturepl.com:** Neil Lucas. **30 Photolibrary:** Karen Gowlett-Holmes (cl) (c). **30–31 NHPA / Photoshot:** Stephen Dalton. **31 Corbis:** Stephen Frink (c); Stuart Westmorland (bc). **32 Dorling Kindersley:** Jan Van Der Voot (cl). **NHPA / Photoshot:** Stephen Kraseman (cr). **33 Alamy Images:** blickwinkel (tl). **Corbis:** W. Wisniewski (b). **34 Getty Images:** Tim Flach (c). **naturepl.com:** Ingo Arndt (fcr); Jorma Luhta (cr); Nature Production (bl). **Photolibrary:** Satoshi Kuribayashi / Nature Production (br). **34–35 FLPA:** Scott Linstead / Minden Pictures. **35 FLPA:** Ariadne Van Zandbergen (clb). **36–37 shahimages.com:** Anup Shah. **40 Alamy Images:** WaterFrame (bc). **Corbis:** DLILLC (cl); Paul Souders (tr). **naturepl.com:** Kim Taylor (c). **40–41 naturepl.com:** Kim Taylor; Kim Taylor (t). **NHPA / Photoshot:** Stephen Dalton (b). **41 naturepl.com:** Kim Taylor (t). **Photolibrary:** Satoshi Kuribayashi / Nature Production (c). **42 Alamy Images:** Scenics & Science (ca). **Corbis:** Gary Bell (cl). **Getty Images:** Stephen Frink (br); Visuals Unlimited (tr); Max Gibbs / Photolibrary (cr). **NHPA / Photoshot:** Taketomo Shiratori (bl). **43 Corbis:** Stuart Westmorland / Science Faction (c). **Dorling Kindersley:** Richard Davies of Oxford Scientific Films (bl) (bc) (br). **44–45 FLPA:** Norbert Wu / Minden Pictures. **46 Photolibrary:** OSF (br). Still Pictures: F. Hecker (tr). **46–47 Corbis:** Frans Lanting. **47 Corbis:** Michael & Patricia Fogden (tl). **NHPA / Photoshot:** Roy Walker (br). Still Pictures: Hecker / Sauer (cra). **48 Corbis:** Michael & Patricia Fogden (fbl); John Giustina (bc); George McCarthy (fbr). **naturepl.com:** David Tipling (bl). **NHPA / Photoshot:** John Shaw (br). **48–49 Andras Meszaros. 50 Alamy Images:** blickwinkel (bc). Igor Siwanowicz: (cl). **50–51 Corbis:** Kimimasa Mayama / Reuters. **51 FLPA:** Thomas Marent / Minden Pictures (crb). **Getty Images:** Jonathon Gale (tl). **Science Photo Library:** Revy. ISM (br). **52–53 FLPA:** Norbert Wu / Minden Pictures. **54 Corbis:** Frans Lanting (tr). Getty Images: Doug Hamilton (cl). **55 Alamy Images:** Maximilian Weinzierl (br). **Corbis:** DLILLC (t); Stuart Westmorland (clb). **56 Ardea:** Jean Paul Ferrero (bl). naturepl.com: Roberto Bubas (cl). **56–57 naturepl.com:** David Tipling. **57 NHPA / Photoshot:** A. N. T. Photo Library (tl). **58 NHPA / Photoshot:** Andy Rouse (tr). **Splashdowndirect.com:** Andre Seale (b). 59 Corbis: John Giustina (cl). **FLPA:** Silvestris Fotoservice (ftl). **Getty Images:** Daryl Balfour (crb); Daniel Cox / Photolibrary (bc); Stan Osolinski / Photolibrary (tc). **NHPA / Photoshot:** Stephen Dalton (tl). **Science Photo Library:** Steve Gschmeissner (bl). **60–61 Corbis:** Martin Harvey. **62 Photolibrary:** Howard Hall (tr). **62–63 Ardea:** Francois Gohier. **63 Alamy Images:** AfriPics.com (cla); Imagestate (ca); Johner Images (tr). **Corbis:** Joe McDonald (br). **Getty Images:** Joe McDonald (c). **64–65 naturepl.com:** Anup Shah. 65 naturepl.com: Jurgen Freund (tr). **NHPA / Photoshot:** John Shaw (tr). **66 Corbis:** George McCarthy. imagequestmarine.com: Peter Batson (tr). **67 Ardea:** D. Parer & E. Parer-Cook (crb). **FLPA:** Imagebroker (tr). Science Photo Library: Power and Syred (clb) (bl). **Wikipedia, The Free Encyclopedia:** (tl). **68 Corbis:** Visuals Unlimited (fbr); Frans Lanting (bl); Erich Kuchling / Westend61 (fbl). **Getty Images:** Visuals Unlimited (bc). Stephen J. Simpson & Gregory A. Sword: (br). **68–69 NHPA / Photoshot:** Kevin Schafer. **70 Corbis:** David Aubrey (bc/grasshopper); W. Perry Conway (fbr); Cornstock (fbl); Joe McDonald (br); Skip Moody – Rainbow / Science Faction (bc/frog). **Dorling Kindersley:** Colin Keates, courtesy of the Natural History Museum, London (c). **70–71 Corbis:** Erich Kuchling / Westend61. **71 Miles Kenzo Kooren:** (bl). naturepl.com: Kim Taylor (br). **Science Photo Library:** Volker Steger (tr). **72–73 NHPA / Photoshot:** Dave Watts. **74 Corbis:** Radius Images (tl). **Getty Images:** Tim Graham Photo Library (crb). **75 Corbis:** Frans Lanting (br); Kevin Schafer (l); Keren Su (bc). **FLPA:** Tui De Roy / Minden Pictures (tr). **76 Corbis:** Visuals Unlimited (cl). **FLPA:** Shem Compion (bl). Getty Images: Visuals Unlimited (cr). **77 naturepl.com:** Dave Watts (tl). **NHPA / Photoshot:** Photo Researchers (l). **78 Alamy Images:** dbimages (l). **naturepl.com:** Nature Production (cr). **78–79 Photolibrary:** Otto Hahn. **79 FLPA:** S & D & K Maslowski (tl); Pete Oxford / Minden Pictures (br). **80 Alamy Images:** Steve Bloom Images (l). **81 Alamy Images:** Bob Gibbons (cl). **naturepl.com:** Michael Durham (cr); Laurent Geslin (crb). Stephen J. Simpson & Gregory A. Sword: (b). **82 FLPA:** Richard Herrmann / Minden Pictures (crb). **Getty Images:** Wim van den Heever (bc). **Photolibrary:** Tobias Bernhard (cl). **82–83 naturepl.com:** Doc White. **83 Corbis:** Visuals Unlimited (bc). **84–85 Alexander Safonov. 86 Science Photo Library:** Eye of Science (cl). **86–87 Corbis:** Peter Johnson (b); James Hager / Robert Harding World Imagery (t). **87 Corbis:** Gallo Images (cl). **naturepl.com:** Elaine Whiteford (br). **88 Corbis:** David A. Northcott (fcl). **FLPA:** Martin B Withers (cl). **imagequestmarine.com:** (cr). **naturepl.com:** Rod Williams (c). **NHPA / Photoshot:** Stephen Dalton (fcr). **88–89 Getty Images:** Pal Hermansen. **90 Corbis:** David A. Northcott (tl); Keren Su (cr). **91 Alamy Images:** Malcolm Schuyl (cl). **National Geographic Stock:** Gerry Ellis / Minden Pictures (r). **92–93 naturepl.com:** Charlie Hamilton-James; Mitsuaki Iwago / Minden Pictures (cr). **94 FLPA:** Mark Moffett / Minden Pictures (tr); Martin B Withers (cl). **naturepl.com:** Bruce Davidson (b). **95 Alexander Safonov:** (t). **96 naturepl.com:** David Shale (t). **NHPA / Photoshot:** A. N. T. Photo Library (bl). **97 National Geographic Stock:** Robert Sisson (tl). **naturepl.com:** Rod Williams (cl). **NHPA / Photoshot:** Stephen Dalton (c). **99 FLPA:** Nigel Cattlin (c); imagebroker (cr); Tui De Roy / Minden Pictures (br). **imagequestmarine.com:** Roger Steene (cl). **100 Corbis:** Steven Kazlowski / Science Faction (c). **Dorling Kindersley:** Frank Greenaway, courtesy of the Natural History Museum, London (ca). **FLPA:** Malcolm Schuyl (tr). **Getty Images:** James Hager (cl). **100–101 Getty Images:** Visuals Unlimited. **101 Corbis:** Tom Brakefield (crb); Ralph A. Clevenger (cr); Michael & Patricia Fogden (cra). **naturepl.com:** Ingo Arndt (br). **102–103 Thomas Marent. 104 Corbis:** Michael & Patricia Fogden (cl). **104–105 Getty Images:** Visuals Unlimited (t). **naturepl.com:** Hans Christoph Kappel (b). **105 Alamy Images:** Brent Ward (cl). **FLPA:** Norbert Wu / Minden Pictures (tr). **naturepl.com:** Barry Mansell (br). **106 Corbis:** Theo Allofs (cl). **Dorling Kindersley:** Jerry Young (cb). **Getty Images:** James Warwick (cr). **106–107 Alamy Images:** blickwinkel. **107 Getty Images:** Nigel Dennis / Gallo Images (cr); Visuals Unlimited (cl). **naturepl.com:** Mark Payne-Gill (tl) (ftr) (tc) (tr). **108 Corbis:** Joe McDonald (bc). **Getty Images:** Don Farrall (cl). **108–109 NHPA / Photoshot:** Stephen Dalton. **109 Corbis:** Dr John D. Cunningham / Visuals Unlimited (crb). **FLPA:** Chris Schenk / FN / Minden Pictures (tr); Visuals Unlimited (br). **Getty Images:** Mattias Klum / National Geographic (tl). **Joey Ciaramitaro / GoodMorningGloucester.com:** (bc). **110 Corbis:** Joe McDonald (fclb); DLILLC (clb). **FLPA:** Hiroya Minakuchi / Minden Pictures (cb). **naturepl.com:** Nick Garbutt (crb); Dave Watts (fcrb). **110–111 Corbis:** DLILLC. **112 Corbis:** Joe McDonald (bl); Fritz Rauschenbach (tc). **113 Corbis:** Martin Harvey (br); Frans Lanting (cr); Joe McDonald (fbr). **Getty Images:** Beverly Joubert / National Geographic (tl); Michael Poliza (fbl); David Trood (cl). **Christian Ziegler:** (bl). **114–115 FLPA:** Chris Newbert / Minden Pictures. **116 Dorling Kindersley:** Frank Greenaway, courtesy of the Natural History Museum, London (tr) (br/cricket); Colin Keates, courtesy of the Natural History Museum, London (br). **NHPA / Photoshot:** Stephen Dalton (bc). **Science Photo Library:** Power and Syred (cl). **117 Corbis:** Frans Lemmens (br); Joe McDonald (tc); DLILLC (cl). **118 Alamy Images:** Danita Delimont (clb). **118–119 Frank Greenaway. 119 FLPA:** Hiroya Minakuchi / Minden Pictures (cra) (bc). **NHPA / Photoshot:** A. N. T. Photo Library (tc). **120 Corbis:** Jack Goldfarb / Design Pics (tr). **121 Getty Images:** Jeff Rotman (bl). **121 Getty Images:** NatPhotos (cr). Ch'ien C. Lee: (tl). **Science Photo Library:** Prof. L. M. Beidler (bl). **122 Alamy Images:** John Warburton-Lee Photography (c). **FLPA:** Jurgen & Christine Sohns (bl). 122–123 naturepl.com: Jose B. Ruiz. **123 FLPA:** R. Dirscherl (ca). **naturepl.com:** Nick Garbutt (br). **124–125 FLPA:** Dembinsky Photo Ass. **126 naturepl.com:** Michael D. Kern (bl); Dave Watts (tc). **127 Getty Images:** Jeff Hunter (br). **NHPA / Photoshot:** Martin Harvey (bl). Stephan Rolfes: (cla). Science Photo Library: Catherine Pouedras / Eurelios (ca). **128 Alamy Images:** Phil Degginger (fbl); blickwinkel (bl). **Getty Images:** Nicole Duplaix / National Geographic (br). **naturepl.com:** Georgette Douwma (fbr); Anup Shah (bc). **128–129 Science Photo Library:** Byron Jorjorian. **130 Alamy Images:** Premaphotos (crb). Corbis: Tom Brakefield (cra); George McCarthy (clb); Joe McDonald (cr). **NHPA / Photoshot:** Anna Henly (cl). **130–131 Alamy Images:** David Fleetham. **131 Alamy Images:** Phil Degginger (cr); Keith M Law (cla) (ca). **Getty Images:** Manoj Shah (tc). **132–133 Corbis:** Paul Souders. **134 Alamy Images:** blickwinkel (cl). **naturepl.com:** Rolf Nussbaumer (bl). **134–135 Getty Images:** Visuals Unlimited. **135 Alamy Images:** Juniors Bildarchiv (cra); Rolf Nussbaumer (clb). **Corbis:** Herbert Zettl (br). **Getty Images:** Visuals Unlimited (tc). **136 naturepl.com:** Solvin Zankl (bc). **shahimages.com:** Anup Shah (cl). **136–137 Alamy Images:** Imagestate (t). **naturepl.com:** Anup Shah (b). **137 Alamy Images:** Lena Ason (cr). **Corbis:** Jonathan Blair (tc); B. Borrell Casals; FLPA (tr). **FLPA:** Ingo Arndt / Minden Pictures (br); Sunset (c). **138 Corbis:** Frans Lanting (tr). **138–139 Corbis:** Arthur Morris (b). **139 Corbis:** Norbert Wu / Science Faction (br). **Getty Images:** Nicole Duplaix / National Geographic (tr). **naturepl.com:** Premaphotos (cla). **140 FLPA:** Matthias Breiter / Minden Pictures (clb). Louis-Marie Preau: (tc). **140–141 Tony Heald. 141 Alamy Images:** All Canada Photos (tl). **FLPA:** Mark Moffett / Minden Pictures (br); Sunset (tc). **naturepl.com:** George McCarthy (cr). **NHPA / Photoshot:** George Bernard (crb). **142–143 Andras Meszaros. 144 Corbis:** Mark A Johnson (tl). **144–145 Corbis:** Juergen Effner. **145 Getty Images:** Oxford Scientific / Photolibrary (tl) (tc). naturepl.com: Georgette Douwma (cl). **Photolibrary:** Eliott Neep (tr); Richard Packwood (cr). **Still Pictures:** Vincent Jean-Christoph / Biosphoto (br). **146 Alamy Images:** cbimages (fclb). **Corbis:** Lightscapes Photography Inc. (crb). **Getty Images:** Frank Lukasseck (clb). **naturepl.com:** David Fleetham (cb). **146–147 Louis-Marie Préau. 147 Getty Images:** Stephen Frink (fcrb). **148 Getty Images:** National Geographic (cl); Oxford Scientific / Photolibrary (bl) (bc) (br). **149 naturepl.com:** Meul / ARCO (tr). **NHPA / Photoshot:** Laurie Campbell (bc). **150–151 Michel Loup. 152 Thomas Marent:** (cl) (c). **Photolibrary:** Paul Kay (bl). **152–153 Thomas Marent. 153 Getty Images:** Visuals Unlimited (cra) (br). National Geographic Stock: Piotr Nasrecki / Minden Pictures (tc). Photolibrary: OSF (cr). **154 naturepl.com:** Rolf Nussbaumer (cl). **154–155 FLPA:** Jurgen & Christine Sohns. **155 Alamy Images:** Andrew Darrington (ca); Alison Thompson (tr). **Corbis:** Michael & Patricia Fogden (cra); Wolfgang Kaehler (cr). **Getty Images:** Oxford Scientific / Photolibrary (crb). **156 Getty Images:** Frank Lukasseck (br); Art Wolfe (tr). **naturepl.com:** Anup Shah (cl). **157 Alamy Images:** cbimages (tl). **Ardea:** D. Parer & E. Parer-Cook (ca). **Dorling Kindersley:** Jerry Young (tc). **naturepl.com:** David Fleetham (br); David Kjaer (bl). **Professor Stewart Nicol:** (cra). **158–159 Getty Images:** Michael Poliza / National Geographic. **160 Alamy Images:** blickwinkel (bl). **Corbis:** Michael Hagedorn (bc); Lightscapes Photography Inc. (c); Lynda Richardson (cra). **NHPA / Photoshot:** Anthony Bannister (br). **160–161 Getty Images:** Manoj Shah. **161 Getty Images:** Alain Christof / Photolibrary (tl). **162 Alamy Images:** Mira (c/bees). Daisy Gilardini: (tr); Mark Moffett / Minden Pictures (bl); Piotr Nasrecki / Minden Pictures (c/termites). **National Geographic Stock:** Mitsuhiko Imamori / Minden Pictures (cl) (bc). **162–163 Corbis:** Bob Krist (br). **163 Getty Images:** Stephen Frink (tr). **164 Corbis:** Ralf Hirschberger / dpa (crb); Koen Van Weel / epa (fcrb); Visuals Unlimited (cb); Boston Museum of Science / Visuals Unlimited (fclb). **Getty Images:** George Grall / National Geographic (clb). **164–165 Getty Images:** Digital Vision. **166 Alamy Images:** Martin Shields (clb/sabre tooth). Corbis: Frans Lanting (br); Sergei Cherkashin / Reuters (clb/mammoth). Dorling Kindersley: Ed Homonylo, courtesy of Dinosaur State Park, Connecticut (cl). **166–167 NHPA / Photoshot:** Stephen Dalton. **167 Corbis:** Jean-Pierre Degas / Hemis (cra) (bc/gorilla); Frans Lanting (ca) (fbl). **Getty Images:** Ira Block / National Geographic (bl); Kevin Schafer (tr); Manoj Shah (bc/gibbon). **168 Corbis:** Brandon D. Cole (cb); Michael & Patricia Fogden (ca); Visuals Unlimited (br); Marty Snyderman (tl); Boston Museum of Science / Visuals Unlimited (cra). **Getty Images:** Nick Norman / National Geographic (bc). **NHPA / Photoshot:** Ross & Diane Armstrong (bl). **169 Corbis:** Ed Murray / Star Ledger (tl); Robert Pickford (cla); Jeffrey L. Rotman (cb) (bl) (br). **Getty Images:** Georgette Douwma (clb); Visuals Unlimited (tc). Photolibrary: Paul Kay (ca). SeaPics.com: Susan Dabritz (tr). **170 Corbis:** Brandon D. Cole (cl); B. Borrell Casals; FLPA (crb); Jeffrey L. Rotman (bl). **Getty Images:** AFP (br); Gary Bell (bc); Stephen Frink (cb); George Grall / National Geographic (tr); Visuals Unlimited (cra). **171 Alamy Images:** Sabena Jane Blackbird (cla). **Getty Images:** Philippe Bourseiller (crb); Justin Lewis (cb); George Grall / National Geographic (ca); Norbert Rosing / National Geographic (tr); Visuals Unlimited (br). **NHPA / Photoshot:** Daniel Heuclin (cra). **172 Corbis:** Michael & Patricia Fogden (crb); Frans Lanting (ca); Robert Pickett (bl). **Getty Images:** Mangiwau (br); Visuals Unlimited (cb); David Tipling (clb). **173 Corbis:** David Aubrey (br); Ashley Cooper (bl); Michael & Patricia Fogden (c); Robert Pickett (tr); Bob Sacha (clb); Bill Vane (tc). **Getty Images:** Thomas Shahan (cl). **174 Corbis:** Michael & Patricia Fogden (bc); Anthony Bannister / Gallo Images (cr); Visuals Unlimited (bl); Frans Lanting (c/stick insect); Naturfoto Honal (tr); David A. Northcott (br); Ken Wilson; Papilio (c/earwig); Mannie Garcia / Reuters (crb); Peet Simard (cl). **Getty Images:** Medford Taylor / National Geographic (cb). **175 Corbis:** David Aubrey (br); Visuals Unlimited (c/flea); George D. Lepp (cl); Robert Marien (cb/butterfly); Micro Discovery (cra); Fritz Rauschenbach (c/horsefly); Elisabeth Sauer (ca/water beetle); Kevin Schafer (tr); Penny Tweedie (cb/ants); Michele Westmorland (bc). **Getty Images:** George Grall / National Geographic (ca/beetle); Christina Bollen / Photolibrary (clb); Robert Oelman / Photolibrary (cla); David R. Tyner (cr). **176 Corbis:** Amos Nachoum (clb). **Getty Images:** Georgette Douwma (crb); Stephen Frink (bl); Jens Kuhfs (br); Darlyne A Murawski / National Geographic (cla); Visuals Unlimited (ca); Jeff Rotman (cr); Michele Westmorland (cb). **177 Getty Images:** Peter David (c/anglerfish); Steven Hunt (cb) (br); Michael Melford (c/salmon); Joel Sartore / National Geographic (tc/sturgeon); Paul Nicklen / National Geographic (cl); Visuals Unlimited (tc/lungfish) (cr) (cra); Luc Novovitch (bl); Jeff Rotman (ca) (bc); Peter Scoones (tl). **178 Corbis:** Jan-Peter Kasper / epa (cb); Michael & Patricia Fogden (cla); Visuals Unlimited (bc). **Getty Images:** Don Farrall (cr); George Grall / National Geographic (clb); Michael Fogden / Photolibrary (crb). **NHPA / Photoshot:** Anthony Bannister (br); Chris Mattison (cra). **179 Corbis:** Michael & Patricia Fogden (cra) (bl) (ca/left); Frans Lanting (cla); moodboard (ca/right); Natural Selection David Spier (c/right); David A. Northcott (clb); Kevin Schafer (tl) (cb) (cr); Paul Sutherland / National Geographic (c). **Getty Images:** Stanley Breeden / National Geographic (tr); Rodger Jackman / Photolibrary (tc). **NHPA / Photoshot:** Daniel Heuclin (cl); Chris Mattison (bc). **180 Corbis:** Ron Austing; FLPA (cb); Michael & Patricia Fogden (br); Frans Lanting (cr); Gerald Nowak / Westend61 (bl); Stuart Westmorland (clb). **Getty Images:** Tim Flach (crb); Frans Lemmens (bc). **181 Corbis:** Theo Allofs (cla); Jonathan Blair (crb); Chris Mattison; FLPA (cb/boa); Michael & Patricia Fogden (tc) (bc/viper); Gallo Images (tl); David A. Northcott (cb/snake); Clive Druett; Papilio (c/right). **Getty Images:** Theo Allofs (clb); Flickr (ca/agama); Belinda Wright / National Geographic (cl); Visuals Unlimited (tr); Nancy Nehring (cr); Michael Fogden / Photolibrary (br); Doug Plummer (ca/frilled); James R. D. Scott (bc). **Rob Houston:** (c/left). **182 Alamy Images:** blickwinkel (br). **Corbis:** Ralf Hirschberger / dpa (clb); Momatiuk-Eastcott (cra) (cr). **Getty Images:** altrendo nature (bc); Robin Bush / Photolibrary (cla); Ronald Wittek (cb); Tim Zurowski (clb). **183 Corbis:** Steve Allen / Brand X (ca/eagle); Christian Hager / dpa (cr); Patrick Pleul / dpa (crb); Frans Lanting (c/pigeon) (cb); Joe McDonald (tr). **Dorling Kindersley:** Steve & Dave Maslowski / Maslowski Photo (clb). **Getty Images:** Glenn Bartley (bc); Guy Edwardes (cl); Martin Harvey (c/macaw); Don Johnston (br); Mike Powles / Photolibrary (tc); Purestock (bl); Rich Thompson (ca/pelicans); Tohoku Colour Agency; Carl D. Walsh (cla). **184 Corbis:** Markus Botzek (br); Ronald Wittek / dpa (clb); Nigel J. Dennis / Gallo Images (c). **Dorling Kindersley:** Jerry Young (tl). Getty Images: Ben Cranke (bl); Karen Desjardin (bc); Paul Sutherland / National Geographic (cr). **185 Corbis:** Frans Lanting (bc); DLILLC (tr); Naturfoto Honal (bl); George Steinmetz (br). **Dorling Kindersley:** Sean Hunter (cb). **Getty Images:** Joel Sartore / National Geographic (cla); Bob Stefko (clb); Federico Veronesi (tl). **186 Corbis:** Erwin & Peggy Bauer (cra); Niall Benvie (tc/hedgehog); W. Perry Conway (crb); DLILLC (bl). **Dorling Kindersley:** Jerry Young (tr). **Getty Images:** Ben Cranke (tc/bat); Berndt Fischer / Photolibrary (clb); Keren Su (b). **187 Corbis:** John Pitcher / Design Pics (tc); Koen Van Weel / epa (cl); John Giustina (bl); Specialist Stock (cr); Stuart Westmorland (br). **Dorling Kindersley:** Stephen Oliver (c). **Getty Images:** Andy Rouse (tr)

Jacket images: *Front:* **Corbis:** Tim Davis t; DLILLC fbr; Norbert Wu / Science Faction bc; Jim Zuckerman fbl; **Getty Images:** Ralph Orlowski br; Steve & Ann Toon bl. *Back:* **Corbis:** Theo Allofs ftr; Terry W. Eggers tr; Arthur Morris tl; Stuart Westmorland tc; **Getty Images:** Georgette Douwma ftl; **naturepl.com:** Staffan Widstrand b. Spine: **Corbis:** Ralph A. Clevenger cb; DLILLC tc; Jim Zuckerman bc; **Getty Images:** Ralph Orlowski ca; Steve & Ann Toon c

All other images © Dorling Kindersley
For further information see: www.dkimages.com